EASY COOKING
for the kitchen apprentice

EASY COOKING
for the kitchen apprentice

Simple steps to kitchen confidence with 75 fabulous recipes for every
occasion, shown in more than 275 stage-by-stage photographs

EDITOR
BRIDGET JONES

southwater

This edition is published by Southwater
an imprint of Anness Publishing Ltd
Blaby Road, Wigston, Leicestershire LE18 4SE
info@anness.com

www.southwaterbooks.com; www.annesspublishing.com

© Anness Publishing Ltd 2012

If you like the images in this book and would like to investigate using them
for publishing, promotions or advertising, please visit our website
www.practicalpictures.com for more information

Publisher: Joanna Lorenz
Editorial Director: Helen Sudell
Editor: Simona Hill
Designer: Ian Sandom
Production Controller: Steve Lang

Photographers: Tim Auty, Martin Brigdale, Nicky Dowey, James Duncan, Dave King, William
Lingwood, Steve Moss, Thomas Odulate, Craig Robertson, Sam Stowell

Recipe writers: Pepita Aris, Catherine Atkinson, Alex Barker, Michelle Berriedale-Johnson,
Angela Boggiano, Kit Chan, Jacqueline Clark, Maxine Clark, Matthew Drennan, Joanna Farrow,
Jenni Fleetwood, Brian Glover, Nicola Graimes, Christine Ingram, Becky Johnson, Bridget
Jones, Lucy Knox, Lesley Mackley, Sally Mansfield, Sallie Morris, Anna Mosesson, Keith
Richmond, Rena Salaman, Anne Sheasby, Christopher Trotter, Linda Tubby, Suzanne Vandyck,
Jenny White, Kate Whiteman, Carol Wilson, Jeni Wright, Annette Yates

A CIP catalogue record for this book is available from the British Library.

Previously published as part of a larger volume, *The Beginner's Easy-to-Use How to Cook Book*

NOTES

Bracketed terms are intended for American readers.

For all recipes, quantities are given in both metric and imperial measures and, where appropri-
ate, in standard cups and spoons. Follow one set of measures, but not a mixture, because they
are not interchangeable.

Standard spoon and cup measures are level. 1 tsp = 5ml, 1 tbsp = 15ml, 1 cup = 250ml/8fl oz.
Australian standard tablespoons are 20ml. Australian readers should use 3 tsp in place of
1 tbsp for measuring small quantities.

American pints are 16fl oz/2 cups. American readers should use 20fl oz/2.5 cups in place of
1 pint when measuring liquids.

Electric oven temperatures in this book are for conventional ovens. When using a fan oven, the
temperature will probably need to be reduced by about 10–20°C/20–40°F. Since ovens vary,
you should check with your manufacturer's instruction book for guidance.

The nutritional analysis given for each recipe is calculated per portion (i.e. serving or item),
unless otherwise stated. If the recipe gives a range, such as Serves 4–6, then the nutritional
analysis will be for the smaller portion size, i.e. 6 servings. Measurements for sodium do not
include salt added to taste.

Medium (US large) eggs are used unless otherwise stated.

Main front cover image shows Spaghetti with Meatballs (see page 78).

PUBLISHER'S NOTE

Although the advice and information in this book are believed to be accurate and true at the
time of going to press, neither the author nor the publisher can accept any legal responsibility or
liability for any errors or omissions that may be made nor for any inaccuracies nor for any harm
or injury that comes about from following instructions or advice in this book.

Contents

Introduction

If you are a novice in the kitchen and would like some simple ideas for making tasty and nutritious food within a reasonable budget, and without spending too much time slaving over a hot stove, then look no further. While some first-time cooks may feel daunted about trying out new techniques, the ideas and recipes here are designed to teach simple skills and make cooking accessible to everyone, including those who don't have that much time, or those with a restricted budget. Most of all, they offer simple, wholesome, tasty dishes for all to enjoy.

WHY COOK?

There are many motivating factors for wanting to prepare your own food. Living alone for the first time and having to cater for yourself, setting up home with a partner, expecting a baby, or wanting to encourage toddlers to eat healthily are all common reasons. Alternatively, suddenly facing an illness or wanting to follow a specific diet may force you to rethink your cooking habits. Maybe instead you're trying to cut down on food bills, or want to avoid using so many plastic-wrapped pre-cooked meals.

Whatever has inspired your desire to cook, there is no doubt that home-made usually tastes better than ready-made and will satisfy your hunger for longer, too. And when you know the ingredients used in each meal that you prepare, then cooking for yourself becomes more appealing.

SIMPLE FIRST STEPS

Learning to shop successfully means buying only the ingredients that are needed, ensuring that they are of a quality suitable for the dishes that you wish to cook, and at a price that you can afford.

Being a good cook does not mean having a vast repertoire of complicated dishes. Start by making the foods that most appeal, such as a hot snack of cheese on toast. Move on to learn to make a cheese omelette and then spaghetti with carbonara sauce. Then you can try making an all-in-one dish, such as cod gratin or cottage pie.

USING THIS BOOK

The information here is presented so that you can dip into different sections and mix and match recipes that appeal, each one extending your repertoire. The cooking methods are planned around a limited preparation time, so complex processes are avoided. There is a sensible attitude to ready-made products, with guidance on the types of food to make or buy, as well as how to use canned and frozen foods that can be quickly turned into high-quality meals.

The book is organized according to ingredient: chapters cover eggs; vegetables; pasta, grains and legumes; fish and shellfish; poultry; meat; and desserts and bakes. Each section provides a range of recipes, all classic dishes, each of them made with a minimum of ingredients. These offer a variety of different cooking styles, as well as meals for different occasions, such as snacks, light lunches, main course meals and quick supper dishes, so you will never be short of delicious food to cook.

Above: A simple idea with great flavours – freshly cooked pasta with green pesto and shavings of Parmesan.

Above: Hot and spicy foods, such as these chickpea samosas, are quick and easy to make.

Above: Simple vegetable combinations, such as carrots and leeks look great and taste wonderful.

Above: Flour is essential for baking and making sauces and is a key store cupboard ingredient.

Above: Eggs are invaluable in the kitchen and can be used to make both sweet and savoury dishes.

Above: Sugar is used in all kinds of baking and preserved dishes. Store it in a clean, dry container.

FOODS TO KEEP IN STOCK

Here are some suggestions for ingredients to always have available.

DRY STORE-CUPBOARD FOODS

Cornflour (cornstarch) is used for thickening, and stores well.

Flour – plain (all-purpose) to use for sauces and thickening.

Self-raising (self-rising) flour for baking cakes and muffins.

Sugar for sweetening and for baking and desserts. Caster (superfine) sugar, granulated (white) sugar and icing (confectioners') sugar.

Dried fruit such as sultanas (golden raisins), raisins, apricots, figs and dates for baking, desserts, salads, stir-fries, casseroles and snacks.

Plain unsalted nuts such as almonds, walnuts, hazelnuts, Brazil nuts, flaked (sliced) almonds, pistachios, and pine nuts for stir-fries, salads, toppings, stuffings, baking and desserts.

Rolled oats and breakfast cereals mixed with dried fruit and/or fresh fruit, make good gratin or crumble toppings.

Pasta, rice, noodles, and grains to serve with a main, or with a sauce.

CANNED FOODS

Canned fish such as tuna, sardines and anchovies are good for salads; baked potatoes; and for making pâtés with soft cheese, toast toppers or sandwich fillings. Tuna is good in savoury white sauces with rice, couscous, pasta or baked potatoes.

Canned beans (pulses) such as red kidney, cannellini beans and chickpeas for casseroles, soups and stir-fries.

Canned vegetables – use tomatoes and corn in casseroles, soups and sauces.

Canned fruit such as peaches, oranges, pineapple and pears, in syrup or juice mix well with fresh and dried fruit to make fruit salads. Use with natural yogurt for breakfast, or with ice cream for a speedy dessert.

BOTTLED ITEMS

Condiments, oils and vinegars – salt, black pepper, extra virgin olive oil, sunflower oil, cider vinegar, dried herbs and spices, mustard, honey and maple syrup are all useful to keep in store. Olive oil and/or sunflower oil is used for cooking and in dressings. Mustard is useful for dressings and sauces. Honey and maple syrup sweeten natural (plain) yogurt, pancakes and ice cream.

REFRIGERATED FOOD

Dairy products such as butter, margarine and natural yogurt form the basics for simple meals. Yogurt is endlessly versatile and used for dips or sweet desserts with fruit and/or syrup.

Vegetables such as tomatoes, (bell) peppers, Chinese cabbage, celery, carrots, long-life vacuum-packed plain beetroot (beet) (without acid or vinegar) are all useful ingredients to use in cooked or uncooked dishes, salads and sandwiches.

Soft summer berries and grapes to use in desserts and salads.

Lemons for flavouring dishes.

Jars of peanut butter, marmalade and fruit preserves have multiple uses, but all need to be chilled once opened. Use peanut butter for dressings and stir-fries and spreading, and marmalade for savoury cooking, desserts and spreading. Use sweet fruit preserves in natural yogurt and for baking and spreading.

FROZEN FOOD

Fish and seafood such as white fish, salmon, smoked haddock and peeled cooked prawns (shrimp) are all available frozen. Fish fillets cook from frozen by baking, grilling (broiling) or poaching. Inexpensive peeled cooked prawns can be cooked again from frozen in sauces or stir-fries or used in bakes. Thawed and drained, they can be added to salads.

Poultry and meat such as thin fillets of turkey breast or chicken, stir-fry strips or finely diced turkey or chicken, diced meat for casseroles and free-flow minced (ground) meat can be cooked from frozen. Use in stir-fries, meaty sauces or casseroles.

Vegetables such as peas, broad (fava) beans, corn, mixed vegetables, chopped cooked spinach and sliced leeks all freeze well. Add to sauces, stews, stir-fries, or just steam to serve alongside the main dish.

Breads that are useful include French, pitta, naan, ciabatta and good-quality pizza bases. Warm bread always makes a good accompaniment to a dish.

Butter and cheese Store these items diced or grated, ready to use.

Eggs

Eggs are so familiar it is easy to forget what an exciting ingredient they can be. They are brilliant for both savoury and sweet cooking, from making the simplest meals to the most stylish concoctions. Not only are they versatile, but they are also inexpensive, full of nutritional value, and quick and easy to cook. Eggs keep well and are an essential item to keep on hand in a cool store cupboard.

Boiled eggs

Eggs should never be boiled rapidly as this frequently causes the shells to crack, and results in whites with a very rubbery texture. Timing is most accurate when eggs are added to water that is simmering steadily or boiling gently. Start timing the cooking when the water is bubbling gently again. This method is good for soft-boiled eggs, when timing is crucial if the white is to be just firm and the yolk runny. Serve with buttered toast cut into fingers.

1 If the eggs have been chilled put them in cold water. Heat the water until bubbling gently, then begin timing the egg.

2 If the eggs are at room temperature, lower them on a spoon into simmering water, taking care not to let them drop on to the base of the pan or they will crack.

3 Cut off the top of the egg with a sharp knife.

COOKING TIMES

Start timing the cooking when the water boils gently. If you start off with hot water, reduce the cooking time by about 30 seconds. Allow an extra 30 seconds for really fresh eggs and more if they are very cold.

Cooking times in minutes

	small	medium	large
Soft	3	4	4½–5
Semi-firm	4	5–6	6–7
Hard	7	8–10	10–12

COOK'S TIPS

• When cooking hard-boiled eggs, cover them with cold water and bring to the boil.

• Timing hard-boiled eggs is not as critical as when cooking a perfect soft-boiled yolk with a white that is softly set. However, over-cooked hard-boiled eggs have rubbery whites and dry crumbly yolks.

• As soon as the water begins to boil, reduce the heat so that the eggs barely simmer. Cook the eggs gently for the recommended time and never leave them to boil for too long.

• As soon as hard-boiled eggs are cooked, drain and crack them, then place them in cold water. This prevents a black ring from forming around the yolk. Shell them when they are cool enough to handle, or to shell them while they are still hot, hold them under cold water to avoid burning your fingers.

• Finally, rinse off any bits of shell before using the eggs. Egg shell is hard and will spoil the dish.

Serving ideas

Egg and potato salad Mix cooked sliced salad potatoes, spring onions (scallions) and mayonnaise and then top with roughly chopped hard-boiled egg. Alternatively, toss halved cooked potatoes and spring onions with oil and vinegar dressing, then mix in the roughly chopped eggs. Chopped canned anchovies and drained capers are good with this salad.

Egg and cherry tomato salad Halved cherry tomatoes, spring onions, lots of chopped parsley and a drizzle of olive oil are fabulous with wedges of hard-boiled egg. Add some sliced black olives and basil for a stylish dish.

Egg and beetroot (beet) salad Cooked plain beetroot is excellent with eggs. Dice the beetroot, top with chopped hard-boiled egg and sprinkle with spring onions. Drizzle with olive oil and sprinkle with pine nuts for a great salad.

Eggs mornay Coat hard-boiled eggs with cheese sauce, sprinkle with grated cheese and grill (broil) until golden. Delicious on a layer of cooked spinach.

Egg curry Add hard-boiled eggs to curry sauce and heat gently. Serve with rice and a raita or spinach. For a dry or slightly moist egg curry, cook an onion in oil or butter, stir in curry or tandoori paste and cook for a few minutes. Add shelled, whole, freshly cooked hard-boiled eggs and stir to coat well. Remove from the heat and stir in a little cream or yogurt and chopped fresh coriander (cilantro). Halve the eggs and serve with rice or naan.

Energy per egg 94kcal/392kJ; Protein 8g; Carbohydrate 0g, of which sugars 0g; Fat 7.1g, of which saturates 2g; Cholesterol 244mg; Calcium 36mg; Fibre 0g; Sodium 90mg.

Scrambled eggs

Scrambled eggs are a quick meal, served simply on toast, warm pitta, plain bagels, or naan bread. Scrambled eggs should be creamy and fluffy – lightly set or slightly thicker, but never firm. They are made by gently heating a mix of eggs and milk and stirring constantly to produce a scrambled effect. Use three eggs for a hearty appetite, less for a quick snack.

Serves one

3 eggs
salt and black pepper
15g/½oz/1 tbsp butter, for cooking

1 Beat the eggs well with a little seasoning until the white and yolk are thoroughly combined.

2 Heat the butter over low to medium heat to melt but do not let it get sizzling hot. Ensure the bottom and lower part of the pan sides are well coated wwith melted butter so that the egg does not stick.

3 Add the egg mixture to the pan and stir frequently over a medium heat for 1–2 minutes, until the eggs are lightly set but still very moist and creamy. Remove from the heat.

4 For more firmly set egg with a drier texture, cook for about 4 minutes.

COOK'S TIPS
• Getting the toast ready on time is vital: beat the eggs, melt the butter in the pan and set it aside, then toast the bread, butter it and place on a warmed plate (a cold plate makes toast soggy). Quickly scramble the eggs. Abandoning the eggs to toast the bread or butter the toast will mean they may overcook or set in a lump. There is a point early on in the setting when a few seconds of not stirring will not cause disaster. With practice, it is easier to toast the bread and butter it while cooking the eggs.
• Cook 1–4 beaten eggs in the microwave for 30 seconds at a time, whisking well each time, until barely set. Stand for 30 seconds.

Serving ideas
• Serve on split warmed croissants with smoked salmon.
• Try them in baked potatoes, sprinkled with cooked ham or peeled cooked prawns (shrimp).
• Stir in grated cheese and sliced spring onions (scallions), or diced ripe tomatoes, just before serving and serve with potato wedges.
• Serve in roasted (bell) peppers, and top with anchovy fillets.
• Stir-fry baby spinach in a little butter or olive oil and spread over soft wheat flour wraps, sprinkle with grated cheese and spring onions and keep warm under the grill (broiler) or in a warm oven on plates while scrambling eggs. Top with scrambled eggs, fold and serve.

Energy 390kcal/1617kJ; Protein 23.8g; Carbohydrate 0g, of which sugars 0g; Fat 33.3g, of which saturates 14g; Cholesterol 758mg; Calcium 111mg; Fibre 0g; Sodium 379mg.

Fried eggs

Super-quick to make, fried eggs are perfect on toast, in a sandwich or served with fried bacon, mushrooms and tomatoes for a filling breakfast. The trick is to work quickly. The fat must be hot enough for the eggs to bubble and cook as soon as they are added to the pan, but not so hot that they break up. Keep watch on the eggs all the time or they will quickly burn.

COOK'S TIPS

• For fast-cooked, slightly crisp-edged fried eggs, a light vegetable oil and a pan that will not stick are essential.

• Olive oil is excellent for shallow frying eggs but at a lower temperature than vegetable oil. The eggs will not fry quite as fast and will produce an evenly set white that is not crispy around the edge. Use just enough to thinly coat the pan and season the eggs with pepper and a hint of salt just before serving.

• Butter is excellent for frying eggs, either alone or with some oil. Do not overheat the fat or it may burn. Do not use too much butter and oil or the eggs will be greasy.

Serves one

1 or 2 eggs
oil, for frying

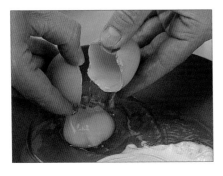

1 Heat 30–45ml/2–3 tbsp oil in a frying pan over medium heat. Crack the egg into the pan and allow it to settle and start bubbling gently around the edges before basting or adding another egg.

2 After about 1 minute, spoon a little hot oil over the white to cook the egg evenly and then over the yolk.

3 Cook until the white has become completely opaque and the edges are just turning bown. For a firmer yolk, cook the egg until the yolk is set, basting it with oil. Use a fish slice or metal spatula to lift the egg out of the pan, carefully allowing oil to drain off.

4 Or, for a firm white and soft yolk, flip the egg over, using a fish slice, as soon as the white has part-set and is firm enough to turn. Cook for 1 minute.

Serving idea
Halve and grill (broil) lots of ripe tomatoes. Sprinkle with a good handful of chopped fresh parsley Serve on toast for a quick supper. Top with eggs fried in olive oil.

Energy per egg 148kcal/613kJ; Protein 8g; Carbohydrate 0g, of which sugars 0g; Fat 13.1g, of which saturates 2.8g; Cholesterol 244mg; Calcium 36mg; Fibre 0g; Sodium 90mg.

Poached eggs

This simple, but delicate cooking method still provokes debate about whether to add vinegar, to make the water swirl causing the egg white to wrap itself around the yolk, or to add the egg and turn off the heat. All are successful in their own way. The most important thing is to use really fresh eggs, otherwise the whites spread into wisps. Serve on buttered toast or muffins.

Serving ideas

Poached eggs are delicious on thick buttery toast, toasted English muffins or crumpets. They are also excellent with grilled (broiled) bacon, sausages, mushrooms and black pudding for a healthier (and less greasy) alternative to fried eggs for a traditional breakfast.
• Coat poached eggs on toast or muffins with a little cheese sauce or hollandaise sauce.
• Serve on poached smoked haddock, with lots of black pepper (cook in separate pans).
• Flavour mashed potatoes with crushed garlic and chopped black olives, adding olive oil instead of butter, and serve topped with a poached egg.
• Spinach and poached eggs are fabulous together – add shavings of Parmesan or finely crumbled feta or blue cheese.
• Serve in a bowl of soup – try spinach, broccoli or pea soup.
• Try poaching an egg in broth: thin broths with vegetables (especially seasoned with spices) are fabulous with egg.
• Serve on basmati rice cooked with peas and drizzle with a little chilli oil.
• Serve poached eggs on freshly cooked pasta shapes mixed with peas or asparagus, and sprinkle with shredded cooked ham and a little Parmesan cheese.
• Turkish-style poached eggs served in a puddle of plain, creamy yogurt are really good – especially sprinkled with herbs, such as chopped fresh coriander (cilantro), parsley and basil. Season with chilli oil and serve with warm bread.

Serves one

2 eggs
15ml/1 tbsp vinegar

1 Pour 2.5–4cm/1–1½in water into a frying pan. Add the vinegar and bring to the boil. Reduce the heat, if necessary, to keep the water bubbling gently.

2 Crack an egg into a cup, then tip it into the water, controlling where you put it in the pan. Add the second egg.

3 Cook the eggs very gently for 1–2 minutes undisturbed. Carefully spoon a little water over the centre of the eggs to cook the yolk.

4 The eggs are cooked when they can be loosened easily from the bottom of the pan. Use a skimmer, draining spoon, fish slice or metal spatula to lift the eggs from the water. Drain the eggs well and place them on a warmed plate. Snip off any scraps of untidy white with scissors before serving.

Energy 188kcal/783kJ; Protein 16g; Carbohydrate 0g, of which sugars 0g; Fat 14.2g, of which saturates 4g; Cholesterol 487mg; Calcium 73mg; Fibre 0g; Sodium 179mg.

Omelettes

Perfect on its own for breakfast, lunch or supper; all sorts of seasonings, fillings or toppings can be added to make an omelette more substantial. Traditionally rolled, or folded to enclose a filling, an omelette can also be served flat and topped with any flavouring ingredients.

2 Cook the eggs for a few seconds until the base has set, then use a fork to push in the sides so that the unset egg runs on to the hot pan. Cook until just beginning to set.

3 Tilt the pan and fold over a third of the omelette using a plastic spatula.

4 Still tilting the pan away from you, flip the omelette over again and slide it out of the pan on to a warmed plate, with the folded sides underneath. Alternatively, an omelette can be folded once, in half. Serve at once.

COOK'S TIPS
• Although special omelette pans are available, any non-stick frying pan will do.
• Prepare the flavourings and fillings first and have a warmed serving plate ready.
• Do not start cooking until you are ready to eat.

Serves one

2 eggs, seasoned with salt and pepper
chopped herbs, if liked
15g/½oz/1 tbsp butter

1 Beat the eggs with the herbs, if using. Heat the butter in a frying pan until very hot, but not smoking. Pour in the eggs, so that they cover the pan base.

BASIC OMELETTE

There are several types of omelette: classic, set or soufflé. This classic omelette is set on the outside, but slightly runny in the middle, with a creamy texture. An omelette makes a quick lunch for a small appetite. Top with cheese, or fill with chopped mushrooms, for more flavour.

Energy 205kcal/854kJ; Protein 9.5g; Carbohydrate 11.9g, of which sugars 11.9g; Fat 13.8g, of which saturates 3g; Cholesterol 285mg; Calcium 49mg; Fibre 0g; Sodium 686mg.

4 Place a plate over the pan. Put your hand firmly on the top, then quickly turn over both pan and plate together.

5 Lift off the pan and allow the omelette to slip out on to the plate. Slide the omelette back into the pan, cooked-side up, and continue cooking until set and golden underneath.

SOUFFLÉ OMELETTE

When the yolks and whites are whisked separately, and the whites folded into the yolks, the result is a soufflé omelette.

Serves one

2 eggs, separated
15g/½oz/1 tbsp butter
chopped strawberries, to serve

1 Beat the yolks in a large bowl. Whisk the whites until stiff, then fold them into the yolks until evenly blended. Heat the grill (broiler) to the hottest setting.

2 Heat the butter in a frying pan, add the eggs and spread out. Cook for 2–3 minutes, until firm underneath. Place under the grill until set and browned on top. Spoon the strawberries over.

TORTILLA

Thick, set omelettes, such as Spanish tortilla or Italian frittata, can be served warm or cold; they can also be cut into small portions to serve as finger food. The mixture is cooked slowly until set.

Serves three

15g/½oz/1 tbsp butter
30ml/2 tbsp oil
1 small potato, thinly sliced
1 small onion, peeled and sliced
6 eggs, separated
salt and ground black pepper
1 garlic clove, crushed
15ml/1 tbsp parsley, chopped
small chunks of vegetable

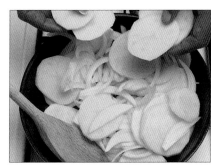

1 Heat a mixture of butter and oil in a large pan. Add the sliced potato and onion and cook gently for about 20 minutes, until tender.

2 Beat the eggs with the seasoning, crushed garlic and chopped parsley. Pour the eggs over the vegetables.

3 Cook gently until the egg has just set. This will take 30 minutes or more. Keep the heat low or the underneath will burn.

Serving ideas
• Grated cheese, finely chopped parsley and/or shredded basil and diced tomato.
• Sliced mushrooms – cook in a little butter or oil first, then remove from the pan while the omelette cooks. Alternatively, leave them in the pan and to set in the omelette.
• Herbs – chopped fresh parsley, dill and tarragon are excellent in omelette; add to the beaten egg. Alternatively, sprinkle shredded basil leaves over before folding, or add chopped coriander (cilantro) before the egg sets.
• Diced cooked ham or salami are good plain, with herbs or cheese.
• Canned tuna mixed with soft cheese and parsley are delicious in plain or soufflé omelettes. For a creamy version, make a little cheese sauce, add drained canned tuna, parsley and chives, then spoon this over the cooked omelette before serving.
• Top a thin, set omelette with shredded ham, chopped spring onions (scallions), tortilla chips and grated cheese. Sprinkle with dried chilli flakes, if liked, and grill (broil) until the cheese is bubbling.
• Sliced mixed red and green (bell) peppers are delicious with sliced olives and spring onions.
• Served with a side salad, an omelette can make a simple snack.
• Include lots of vegetables and serve the omelette with hot crusty bread, new potatoes, a spoonful of creamy mash or instant couscous for a substantial meal.

Omelette Energy 377kcal/1570kJ; Protein 19g; Carbohydrate 14.9g, of which sugars 14.8g; Fat 27g, of which saturates 9.2g; Cholesterol 405mg; Calcium 249mg; Fibre 0.3g; Sodium 648mg.
Tortilla Energy 163kcal/682kJ; Protein 5.8g; Carbohydrate 14.7g, of which sugars 2.8g; Fat 9.5g, of which saturates 1.9g; Cholesterol 127mg; Calcium 32mg; Fibre 1.2g; Sodium 56mg.

Pancakes

A batter is a mixture of flour and a liquid, such as milk and eggs. It can be used to make any number of wonderful dishes from thin French crêpes, large pancakes or small, thick drop scones (with a raising agent added) and baked specialities, such as Yorkshire pudding. Serve with either jam, sugar, golden syrup, lemon juice, currants, sultanas or raisins.

Serves four

225g/8oz/2 cups plain (all-purpose) flour
2 eggs, beaten
pinch of salt
300ml/½ pint/1¼ cups milk
butter for frying

1 Put half of the flour in a bowl with the beaten eggs and beat until the mixture is too thick to continue. There is no need to sift the flour.

2 Add a small quantity of milk to slacken the mixture and continue to beat.

3 Add the remaining flour and beat to a paste.

4 Gradually add the remaining milk and beat until smooth. Set aside to rest for 20 minutes. Stir well before using.

5 Preheat a pan over a medium heat.

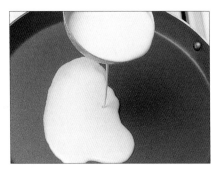

6 Melt a small knob of butter in the frying pan. Turn so the entire base of the pan is coated and sizzling gently. Add a small ladleful of batter.

7 Swirl the batter quickly around the pan to completely coat it. Cook for a minute or so until the underside is golden.

8 With a wide spatula, flip the pancake over and cook the other side for a minute until browned.

Serving idea
Serve pancakes with savoury fillings too – cheese or mushroom sauce work well.

Energy 84kcal/352kJ; Protein 2.8g; Carbohydrate 13g, of which sugars 0.8g; Fat 2.7g, of which saturates 1.3g; Cholesterol 32mg; Calcium 40mg; Fibre 0.5g; Sodium 26mg.

Baked eggs with lentils

This unusual dish makes an excellent vegetarian brunch or supper, served with naan bread. It's a flavourful combination that is filling and delicious. If you prefer, bake the purée and eggs in one large baking dish, making a well in the lentils to accommodate each egg – though you may need to add more baking time to the dish.

Serves four

450g/1lb/2 cups red lentils
3 small leeks, thinly sliced
10ml/2tsp coriander seeds, finely crushed
15ml/1 tbsp chopped fresh
   coriander (cilantro)
30ml/2 tbsp chopped fresh mint
15ml/1 tbsp red wine vinegar
1 litre/1¾ pints/4 cups vegetable stock
sea salt and ground black pepper
4 eggs
generous handful of fresh parsley,
   chopped, to garnish

3 Using the back of a spoon, make a hollow in the lentil mixture in each dish. Break an egg into each hollow. Cover the dishes with foil and bake for 15–20 minutes or until the eggs are set. Srpinkle with plenty of chopped parsley and serve at once.

1 Put the lentils in a deep pan. Add the leeks, coriander seeds, fresh coriander, mint, vinegar and stock. Bring to the boil, then lower the heat and simmer for 30–40 minutes or until the lentils are cooked and have absorbed all the liquid.

2 Preheat the oven to 180°C/350°F/ Gas 4. Season the lentils with salt and pepper and mix well. Spread out in four lightly greased baking dishes.

Variation
Athe end of step 1, add a 400g/14oz can of unsweetened chestnut purée to the lentil mixture and stir well, if you like. Continue as in the main recipe.

Energy 480kcal/2033kJ; Protein 37g; Carbohydrate 67g, of which sugars 5g; Fat 9g, of which saturates 2g; Cholesterol 232mg; Calcium 132mg; Fibre 15g; Sodium 549mg.

Avgolemono

This Greek recipe is a fine example of how a few ingredients can make a marvellous dish. The base of the soup is stock, so choose a well-flavoured one - vegetable stock can be substituted for vegetarian diners. This soup can vary between thick, or broth-like consistency.

Serves four

900ml/1½ pints/3¾ cups chicken stock, preferably home-made
50g/2oz/generous ⅓ cup long grain rice, washed and drained
salt and ground black pepper
3 egg yolks
30–60ml/2–4 tbsp lemon juice
30ml/2 tbsp finely chopped parsley
lemon slices and parsley sprigs, to garnish

1 Pour the stock into a pan, bring to simmering point, then add the drained rice. Half cover and cook for about 12 minutes until the rice is just ender. Season with salt and pepper.

2 Whisk the egg yolks in a bowl, then add about 30ml/2 tbsp of the lemon juice, whisking constantly until the mixture is smooth and bubbly. Add a ladleful of soup and whisk again.

3 Remove the soup from the heat and slowly add the egg mixture, whisking all the time. The soup will thicken slightly.

4 Taste and add more lemon juice if necessary. Stir in the parsley. Serve at once, without reheating, garnished with lemon slices and parsley sprigs.

Cook's tip
The trick with this recipe is to add the egg mixture to the soup without it curdling. Avoid whisking the mixture into boiling liquid and remove the soup from the heat entirely before whisking in the mixture in a slow, steady stream. Do not reheat.

Energy 104kcal/438kJ; Protein 5.5g; Carbohydrate 14.3g, of which sugars 0.7g; Fat 3.2g, of which saturates 0.8g; Cholesterol 95mg; Calcium 20mg; Fibre 0.6g; Sodium 117mg.

Easy cheese soufflé

A light, delicate, melt-in-the-mouth cheese soufflé makes one of the most delightful brunches imaginable. Soufflés are quick to make, but be sure to serve it immediately it is baked, otherwise it may start to sink slightly.

Serves two to three

50g/2oz/¼ cup butter
30–45ml/2–3tbsp dried, fine breadcrumbs
200ml/7fl oz/scant 1 cup milk
30g/1 oz/3 tbsp plain (all-purpose) flour
pinch of cayenne pepper
2.5ml/½ tsp mustard powder
50g/2oz/½ cup mature Cheddar cheese, grated
25g/1oz/⅓ cup freshly grated
   Parmesan cheese
4 eggs, separated, plus 1 egg white
salt and ground black pepper

1 Preheat the oven to 190°C/375°F/ Gas 5.

2 Melt 15ml/1 tbsp of the butter and use to thoroughly grease a 1.2 litre/ 2 pint/5 cup soufflé dish. Coat the inside of the dish with breadcrumbs.

3 Heat the milk in a large pan. Add the remaining butter, flour and cayenne, with the mustard powder. Bring to the boil over a low heat, whisking steadily, until it thickens to a smooth sauce.

4 Simmer the sauce for a minute or two, then turn off the heat and whisk in all the Cheddar and half the Parmesan. Cool a little, then beat in the egg yolks. Check the seasoning; the mixture should be well seasoned. Set aside.

5 Whisk the egg whites in a large grease-free bowl until they form soft, glossy peaks. Do not overbeat or the whites will become grainy and difficult to fold in.

6 Add a few spoonfuls of the beaten egg whites to the sauce to lighten it. Beat well, then tip the rest of the whites into the mixture and, with a large metal spoon, gently fold them in.

7 Pour the mixture into the prepared soufflé dish, level the top and, to help the soufflé rise evenly, run your finger around the inside rim of the dish.

8 Place the dish on a baking sheet. Sprinkle the remaining Parmesan over the top of the soufflé mixture and bake for about 25 minutes until risen and golden brown. Serve immediately, or the soufflé may begin to sink.

Energy 449kcal/1868kJ; Protein 22g; Carbohydrate 15g, of which sugars 4g; Fat 34g, of which saturates 18g; Cholesterol 378mg; Calcium 360mg; Fibre 1g; Sodium 468mg.

Vegetables

Vegetables are essential to our diet. They contribute colour and texture to our meals, making food visually appealing, even when cooked by the most basic of methods. They provide vital flavour to many savoury dishes as well as adding nutritional value. Imagine a casserole without an onion, even if only to flavour the stock or cooking liquid. Vegetables can be cooked by a whole host of methods, with each subtly affecting and adding to the taste of the dish.

Garlicky roasties

Potatoes roasted in their skins retain a deep, earthy taste (and absorb less fat, too) while the garlic mellows on cooking to give a pungent but not overly-strong taste to serve alongside or squeezed over as a garnish. Serve with a traditional roast joint.

Serves four

1kg/2¼lb small floury potatoes
60–75ml/4–5 tbsp sunflower oil
10ml/2 tsp walnut oil
2 whole garlic bulbs, skins left on
salt

1 Preheat the oven to 220ºC/425ºF/ Gas 7. Place the potatoes in a pan of cold water and bring to the boil. Drain.

2 Combine the oils in a roasting pan and place in the oven to get really hot.

3 Add the potatoes and garlic and coat in oil. Roast for 45 minutes until golden.

Energy 312kcal/1310kJ; Protein 6.2g; Carbohydrate 44.3g, of which sugars 3.7g; Fat 13.4g, of which saturates 1.7g; Cholesterol 0mg; Calcium 20mg; Fibre 3.5g; Sodium 29mg.

Oven-roast wedges

This easy alternative to fried chips tastes as good and is much easier to cook. Cut the potatoes into relatively thin sticks or go for great big wedges and allow a little extra cooking time.
To save washing up, lay non-stick baking parchment in the roasting pan, but don't preheat it.

Serves four to six

olive oil
4 medium to large baking potatoes
5ml/1 tsp mixed dried herbs (optional)
sea salt flakes
mayonnaise, to serve

1 Preheat the oven to the highest temperature, 240ºC/475ºF/Gas 9.

2 Lightly oil a large shallow roasting pan and place it in the oven to get really hot while you prepare the potatoes.

3 Cut the potatoes in half and then into long thin wedges. Rinse and dry the potatoes on a dish towel, then place in a bowl or plastic bag and toss in a little oil to coat them evenly.

4 When the oven is really hot, remove the pan carefully and scatter the potato wedges over it, spreading them out in a single layer over the hot oil.

5 Sprinkle with the herbs and salt and roast for about 20 minutes, until golden brown. Remove from the oven and serve with a dollop of mayonnaise.

Energy 377kcal/1589kJ; Protein 6.7g; Carbohydrate 58.9g, of which sugars 2.9g; Fat 14.4g, of which saturates 3.5g; Cholesterol 5mg; Calcium 24mg; Fibre 3.8g; Sodium 30mg.

Irish mashed potatoes

Simple but unbelievably tasty, this traditional Irish way with mashed potatoes makes an excellent companion for a hearty stew of lamb or beef. When it is not accompanying a hearty main dish, it is scrumptious topped with crumbled blue cheese, with a salad on the side.

Serves four

900g/2lb potatoes
1 small bunch spring onions (scallions), finely chopped
150ml/¼ pint/⅔ cup milk
50g/2oz/4 tbsp butter
salt and ground black pepper

1 Cut the potatoes up into chunks. Place in a large pan and cook in boiling water for 15–20 minutes or until tender.

2 Meanwhile, put the spring onions into a pan with the milk. Bring to the boil, then reduce the heat and simmer for about 5 minutes, stirring occasionally, until the spring onions are just tender.

3 Drain the potatoes well and leave to cool. When they are cool enough to handle, peel and return to the pan. Put the pan on the heat and, using a wooden spoon, stir for 1 minute until the moisture has evaporated. Remove the pan from the heat.

4 Mash the potatoes until they are smooth. Then pour in the milk and spring onions and mash until thoroughly combined. Taste and add seasoning, if liked. Serve hot, making a dent in each mound and adding a pool of melted butter to each portion.

COOK'S TIP
For speed and ease, peel the potatoes before step 1. Cut them into small chunks and reduce the cooking time to 10 minutes.

Energy 334kcal/1415kJ; Protein 13.2g; Carbohydrate 66.6g, of which sugars 10.5g; Fat 3.5g, of which saturates 1.7g; Cholesterol 9mg; Calcium 217mg; Fibre 5.2g; Sodium 92mg.

Baked potatoes and three fillings

Potatoes, baked in their skins until they are crisp on the outside and fluffy in the middle, make an excellent and nourishing meal when finished with a simple filling, such as chilli con carne, baked beans or tomatoes and cheese. Try one of these delicious fillings for a super supper.

Serves four

4 medium baking potatoes
olive oil
sea salt
filling of your choice (see below)

1 Preheat the oven to 200°C/400°F/ Gas 6. Score the potatoes with a cross and rub all over with the olive oil.

2 Place on a baking sheet and cook for at least 1 hour until a knife inserted into the centres indicates they are cooked.

COOK'S TIPS
• For even cooking choose potatoes that are similar sizes with undamaged skins and scrub them well, removing any black eyes.
• If the potatoes are cooked before you are ready, remove from the oven. Reheat later in the microwave.

3 Cut the potatoes open and push up the flesh. Season and fill.

STIR-FRIED VEGETABLES
A sweet and sharp-tasting filling.

45ml/3 tbsp groundnut (peanut) or
    sunflower oil
2 leeks, thinly sliced
2 carrots, cut into sticks
1 courgette (zucchini), thinly sliced
115g/4oz baby corn, halved
115g/4oz/1½ cup button (white)
    mushrooms, sliced
45ml/3 tbsp soy sauce
30ml/2 tbsp dry sherry or vermouth
sesame seeds, to garnish

1 Heat the oil in a frying pan. Add the leeks, carrots, courgette and baby corn and stir-fry for about 2 minutes. Add the mushrooms. Stir-fry for 1 minute.

2 Mix the liquids and pour over the vegetables. Heat until just bubbling and scatter over the sesame seeds.

RED BEAN CHILLIES
A filling combination of cheese and beans with additional spicy heat.

425g/15oz can red kidney beans, drained
200g/7oz/scant 1 cup cottage or
    cream cheese
30ml/2 tbsp mild chilli sauce
5ml/1 tsp ground cumin

1 Heat the beans in a pan and stir in the cheese, chilli sauce and cumin.

CHEESE AND CREAMY CORN
A mild and flavoursome topping that is filling, too.

425g/15oz can creamed corn
115g/4oz/1 cup Cheddar cheese, grated
5ml/1 tsp mixed dried herbs
fresh parsley sprigs, to garnish

1 Heat the corn gently until bubbling. Stir in the cheese and mixed herbs until thoroughly combined. Use to fill the potatoes and garnish with parsley.

Energy 223kcal/941kJ; Protein 7.3g; Carbohydrate 38.6g, of which sugars 8.3g; Fat 4.5g, of which saturates 0.8g; Cholesterol 0mg; Calcium 55mg; Fibre 5.4g; Sodium 1150mg.

Braised red cabbage

Lightly spiced with a sharp, sweet flavour, slow cooked braised red cabbage goes well with roast pork, duck and game dishes. It is also delicious with baked ham or crisp, well-browned sausages (garlicky sausages are great) or lamb kebabs.

3 Layer the shredded cabbage in an ovenproof dish with the onions, apples, spices, sugar and seasoning. Pour over the vinegar and add the diced butter.

4 Cover with a lid and cook in the oven for 1½ hours, stirring a couple of times, until the cabbage is very tender. Serve immediately, garnished with the parsley.

Serves four to six

1kg/2¼lb red cabbage
2 cooking apples
2 onions, chopped
5ml/1 tsp freshly grated nutmeg
1.5ml/¼ tsp ground cloves
1.5ml/¼ tsp ground cinnamon
15ml/1 tbsp soft dark brown sugar
45ml/3 tbsp red wine vinegar
25g/1oz/2 tbsp butter, diced
salt and ground black pepper
chopped flat leaf parsley, to garnish

1 Preheat the oven to 160°C/325°F/ Gas 3.

2 Cut away and discard the large white ribs from the outer cabbage leaves using a large, sharp knife, then finely shred the cabbage. Peel, core and coarsely grate the apples.

COOK'S TIPS
• This dish can be cooked in advance and reheated on top of the stove, stirring frequently.
• The cabbage can be braised on top of the stove in a large heavy pan that will not burn. Cook the onions in a little oil first, allowing about 5 minutes so they are soft, but not browned. Add all the other ingredients plus 60ml/4 tbsp water. Bring to the boil, cover, reduce the heat to low and cook gently for 1 hour, stirring occasionally.

Energy 161kcal/669kJ; Protein 2.3g; Carbohydrate 5.8g, of which sugars 5.5g; Fat 14.6g, of which saturates 2.2g; Cholesterol 0mg; Calcium 37mg; Fibre 3.7g; Sodium 15mg.

Roast beetroot

The sweet flavour of beetroot is enhanced by slow roasting. Tangy horseradish and vinegar in cream contrast well with the sweet vegetable. Good with roast beef or venison, the beetroot is also excellent with grilled halloumi cheese or with crumbled feta and lots of crusty bread.

Serves four to six

10–12 small whole beetroot (beet)
30ml/2 tbsp oil
45ml/3 tbsp grated fresh horeseradish
15ml/1 tbsp white wine vinegar
10ml/2 tsp caster (superfine) sugar
150ml/½ pint/⅔ cup double (heavy) cream
salt

COOK'S TIPS
• If you are unable to find fresh horseradish root use preserved grated horseradish instead.
• For a sauce that is lighter in calories, replace the double (heavy) cream with Greek (US strained plain) yogurt.

1 Preheat the oven to 180°C/350°F/ Gas 4. Wash the beetroot without breaking their skins. Trim the stalks to 2.5cm/1in long.

2 Toss the beetroot in the oil and sprinkle with salt. Spread on a roasting pan and cover with foil. Cook for 1½ hours. Leave covered for 10 minutes.

3 To make the horseradish sauce, put the horseradish, vinegar and sugar into a bowl and mix well. Whisk the cream until stiff and fold in the horseradish mixture. Cover and chill until required.

4 When the beetroot are cool enough to handle, slip off the skins and serve with the sauce.

Energy 254kcal/1052kJ; Protein 2.1g; Carbohydrate 10g, of which sugars 9.1g; Fat 22.2g, of which saturates 3.2g; Cholesterol 1mg; Calcium 26mg; Fibre 2.3g; Sodium 143mg.

Peas with lettuce and onion

This is one of those classic dishes that sounds odd to the uninitiated but tastes excellent. Fresh peas vary enormously in the time they take to cook. The tastiest and sweetest are young and freshly picked. Frozen peas need less cooking time and are ready in minutes.

Serves four to six

15g/½oz/1 tbsp butter
1 small onion, finely chopped
1 small round (butterhead) lettuce
450g/1lb/3½ cups shelled fresh peas
    (from about 1.5kg/3½lb peas),
    or frozen peas
45ml/3 tbsp water
salt and ground black pepper

1 Melt the butter in a heavy pan until sizzling. Add the onion and cook over a medium-low heat, stirring once or twice, for about 3 minutes until just softened. Do not allow the onion to brown.

2 Cut the lettuce in half through the core, then place cut side down on a board and slice into thin strips. Place the lettuce strips on top of the onion and add the peas and water. Season lightly with salt and pepper.

3 Bring to the boil, then reduce the heat and cover the pan tightly. Cook over a low heat until the peas are tender – fresh peas will take 10–20 minutes, frozen peas about 5 minutes. Serve piping hot.

Energy 161kcal/670kJ; Protein 9g; Carbohydrate 15.9g, of which sugars 6.8g; Fat 7.4g, of which saturates 3.7g; Cholesterol 13mg; Calcium 73mg; Fibre 6.5g; Sodium 47mg.

Braised leeks with carrots

Sweet carrots and leeks go well together and are good finished with a little chopped mint, chervil or parsley. They complement roast or grilled meat, poultry or sausages and are delicious with boiled ham (home-made or bought) or simply tossed with flaked smoked mackerel.

Serves four

65g/2½oz/5 tbsp butter
675g/1½lb carrots, thickly sliced
2 fresh bay leaves
5ml/1 tsp caster (superfine) sugar
75ml/5 tbsp water
675g/1½lb leeks, cut into 5cm/2in lengths
120ml/4fl oz/½ cup white wine
30ml/2 tbsp chopped fresh mint, chervil
    or parsley
salt and ground black pepper

1 Melt 25g/1oz/2 tbsp of the butter in a pan and cook the carrots gently, without allowing them to brown, for 4–5 minutes.

2 Add the bay leaves, seasoning, sugar and water. Bring to the boil, cover and cook for about 5 minutes, until the carrots are tender. Uncover and then boil until the juices have evaporated, leaving the carrots moist and glazed.

Variations
• For a speedy alternative, use 2 bunches spring onions (scallions) instead of leeks. Slice and stir-fry them in a little butter or oil for about 2 minutes, then add them to the cooked carrots with the herbs.
• To make leeks in tarragon cream cook 900g/2lb leeks in 40g/1½oz/ 3 tbsp butter as above. Season, add a pinch of sugar, 45ml/3 tbsp tarragon vinegar, 6 fresh tarragon sprigs or 5ml/1 tsp dried tarragon and 60ml/4 tbsp white wine. Cover and cook as above. Add 150ml/ ¼ pint/⅔ cup double (heavy) cream and allow to bubble and thicken. Season and serve sprinkled with chopped fresh tarragon. A spoonful of tarragon-flavoured mustard is good stirred into the leeks.

3 Melt 25g/1oz/2 tbsp of the remaining butter in a wide pan or deep frying pan that will take the leeks in a single layer. Add the leeks and fry them in the butter over a low heat for 4–5 minutes, without allowing them to brown.

4 Add seasoning, a good pinch of sugar, the wine and half the chopped herb. Heat until simmering, then cover and cook gently for 5–8 minutes, until the leeks are tender, but not collapsed.

5 Uncover the leeks and turn them in the buttery juices. Increase the heat and then boil the liquid rapidly until reduced to a few tablespoons.

6 Add the carrots to the leeks and reheat them gently, then swirl in the remaining butter. Taste and adjust the seasoning, if necessary. Transfer to a warmed serving dish and serve sprinkled with the remaining chopped herbs.

Energy 163kcal/677kJ; Protein 3.8g; Carbohydrate 18.5g, of which sugars 16.4g; Fat 6.5g, of which saturates 3.6g; Cholesterol 13mg; Calcium 87mg; Fibre 7.8g; Sodium 85mg.

Carrot and coriander soup

Soups are easy to make and a good way to use up vegetables. The preparation time is spent chopping the vegetables. Carrot and coriander are a good flavour combination, and this is one of the most popular soup recipes – perfect for everyday eating. Serve with crusty bread.

Serves four

450g/1lb carrots, preferably young
 and tender
15ml/1 tbsp sunflower oil
40g/1½oz/3 tbsp butter
1 onion, chopped
1 stick celery, plus 2–3 pale leafy tops
2 small potatoes
900ml/1½ pints/3¾ cups vegetable or
 chicken stock
10ml/2 tsp ground coriander
15ml/1 tbsp chopped fresh coriander (cilantro)
150ml/¼ pint/⅔ cup milk
salt and ground black pepper

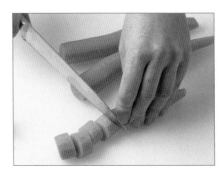

1 Trim and peel the carrots and cut into chunks. Heat the oil and two-thirds of the butter in a pan and fry the onion over medium heat for 3–4 minutes until slightly softened but not brown.

2 Slice the celery and chop the potatoes. Add the celery, potatoes and carrot to the onion and cook for a further 5 minutes, stirring occasionally.

3 Pour in the stock and bring to the boil. Reduce the heat, cover the pan and simmer the soup for about 30 minutes, or until the vegetables are soft.

4 Reserve 6–8 tiny celery leaves from the leafy tops for the garnish, then finely chop the remaining celery tops. Melt the remaining butter in a frying pan and add the ground coriander. Fry for about 1 minute, stirring constantly.

5 Reduce the heat under the pan and add the chopped celery tops and fresh coriander. Fry for about 30 seconds, then remove the pan from the heat.

6 Ladle the soup into a food processor or blender and process until smooth. Pour the soup back into the pan, add the celery tops and coriander. Stir in the milk and heat gently without boiling. Taste for seasoning and add salt and pepper, then serve garnished with the reserved celery leaves.

COOK'S TIP
The amount of salt and pepper to add depends on the type of stock used as well as personal taste.

Energy 168Kcal/697kJ; Protein 3g; Carbohydrate 11.9g, of which sugars 9.2g; Fat 12.4g, of which saturates 6g; Cholesterol 24mg; Calcium 94mg; Fibre 3.1g; Sodium 758mg.

Roasted root vegetable soup

This is a more complex soup involving another cooking stage, but well worth it because roasted vegetables gives a wonderful depth of flavour to soup. You can add other vegetables, such as pumpkin, or use chicken or ham stock in place of vegetable stock. Serve with brown bread.

Serves six

50ml/2fl oz/¼ cup olive oil
1 small butternut squash, seeded and cubed
2 carrots, cut into thick rounds
1 large parsnip, cubed
1 small swede (rutabaga), cubed
2 leeks, thickly sliced
1 onion, quartered
3 bay leaves
4 thyme sprigs, plus extra to garnish
3 rosemary sprigs
1.2 litres/2 pints/5 cups vegetable stock
salt and ground black pepper
soured cream, to serve

1 Preheat the oven to 200°C/400°F/ Gas 6. Put the olive oil into a large bowl. Add the prepared vegetables and toss until coated in the oil.

2 Spread out the vegetables in a single layer on one large or two small baking sheets. Tuck the bay leaves, thyme and rosemary sprigs among the vegetables.

COOK'S TIP
This nutritious soup is good for cold days. The root vegetables contain filling carbohydrates that will help to make you feel full for longer. Make a batch and freeze any leftovers in portions, once it has gone cold. Label each with the soup name and date of freezing.

3 Roast the vegetables for about 50 minutes until tender, turning them occasionally to make sure they brown evenly. Remove from the oven, discard the herbs and transfer the vegetables to a large pan.

Variation
Dried herbs can be used in place of fresh; use 2.5ml/½ tsp of each type.

4 Pour the stock into the pan and bring to the boil. Reduce the heat, season to taste, and then simmer for 10 minutes. Transfer the soup to a food processor or blender (or use a hand blender) and process for a few minutes until thick and smooth.

5 Return the soup to the pan to heat through. Season and serve with a swirl of soured cream. Garnish each serving with a sprig of thyme.

Energy 134kcal/563kJ; Protein 3g; Carbohydrate 17.2g, of which sugars 11.3g; Fat 6.5g, of which saturates 0.9g; Cholesterol 0mg; Calcium 96mg; Fibre 5.2g; Sodium 160mg.

Grilled vegetable pizza

Home-made pizza is far healthier than bought, with the topping of traditional Mediterranean vegetables, plum tomatoes and flavoursome basil and a non-traditional dough base.

4 Place the dough on a sheet of baking parchment on a baking sheet and roll or press it out to form a 25cm/10in round, making the edges slightly thicker than the centre.

5 Brush the pizza dough with any remaining oil, then spread the chopped tomatoes over the dough.

6 Sprinkle chopped basil on top and season with salt and pepper. Arrange the grilled (broiled) vegetables over the herbs and top with the cheese.

7 Bake for 25–30 minutes until crisp and golden brown. Garnish with fresh basil and serve cut into slices.

Serves six

1 courgette (zucchini), sliced
1 small aubergine (eggplant), sliced
30ml/2 tbsp olive oil
1 yellow (bell) pepper, seeded and sliced
115g/4oz/1 cup plain (all-purpose) flour
115g/4oz/1 cup wholemeal
  (whole-wheat) flour
5ml/1 tsp baking powder
pinch of salt
50g/2oz/4 tbsp butter
105ml/7 tbsp milk
4 plum tomatoes, skinned and chopped
30ml/2 tbsp chopped fresh basil
115g/4oz mozzarella cheese, sliced
salt and ground black pepper
fresh basil sprigs, to garnish

1 Preheat the grill (broiler). Brush the courgette and aubergine slices with a little oil and place on a grill rack with the pepper slices. Cook under the grill until lightly browned, turning once.

2 Meanwhile, preheat the oven to 200°C/400°F/Gas 6. Place the plain and wholemeal flours, baking powder and salt in a mixing bowl and stir to mix.

3 Lightly rub in the butter until the mixture resembles coarse breadcrumbs. This can also be done in the food processor. Gradually stir in enough of the milk to make a soft, but not sticky, dough.

COOK'S TIP
If it is more convenient, the vegetables can be prepared in advance. Slice and grill (broil) them and then store in a covered bowl, in the refrigerator, for up to 2 days.

Energy 400kcal/1666kJ; Protein 11.9g; Carbohydrate 34.6g, of which sugars 9.6g; Fat 23.9g, of which saturates 5.3g; Cholesterol 18mg; Calcium 166mg; Fibre 4.4g; Sodium 240mg.

Vegetable tortilla parcels

Seeded green chillies add just a flicker of fire to the spicy tomato filling in these tasty shallow-fried parcels, which are perfect as a main course with salad and potato wedges, or as a snack.

Serves four

675g/1½lb tomatoes
60ml/4 tbsp sunflower oil
1 large onion, finely sliced
1 garlic clove, crushed
10ml/2 tsp cumin seeds
2 fresh green chillies, seeded and chopped
30ml/2 tbsp tomato purée (paste)
1 vegetable stock (bouillon) cube
200g/7oz can corn, drained
15ml/1 tbsp chopped fresh coriander (cilantro)
115g/4oz/1 cup grated Cheddar cheese
8 wheat tortillas
fresh coriander (cilantro), shredded lettuce
and soured cream, to serve

1 To skin the tomatoes, make a small cross with a sharp knife in the bottom of each. Place them in a heatproof bowl, add boiling water to cover and leave for 30 seconds. Lift out with a slotted spoon. Slip the skins off the tomatoes and chop the flesh.

2 Heat half the oil in a frying pan and fry the onion with the garlic and cumin seeds for 5 minutes, until the onion softens. Add the chillies and tomatoes, then stir in the tomato purée.

3 Crumble the stock cube over, stir, and cook gently for 5 minutes, until the chilli is soft but the tomato has not completely broken down. Stir in the corn and coriander and warm through. Keep warm.

COOK'S TIPS
• Mexican wheat tortillas (sometimes described as wheatflour tortillas or wraps) are available in supermarkets.
• Some packets are long-life and will keep for weeks (check the use-by date). They freeze well, are easy to separate and thaw quickly.

4 Sprinkle a little grated cheese in the middle of each tortilla. Spoon some tomato mixture evenly over the cheese. Fold over one edge of the tortilla, then fold over the sides and finally fold up the remaining edge, to enclose the filling completely.

5 Heat the remaining oil in a frying pan and fry the filled tortillas for 1–2 minutes on each side until golden and crisp. Lift them out carefully with tongs and drain on kitchen paper. Serve immediately, with coriander, shredded lettuce and soured cream.

Energy 484kcal/2030kJ; Protein 15.3g; Carbohydrate 58.3g, of which sugars 17.6g; Fat 22.4g, of which saturates 7.9g; Cholesterol 28mg; Calcium 313mg; Fibre 5.4g; Sodium 684mg.

Vegetable korma

Kormas are rich, creamy and subtly spiced one-pot dishes, and this is a delicious example. It is good with plain spiced grilled chicken or fish, or excellent as a meat-free main course.

Serves four

50g/2oz/¼ cup butter
2 onions, sliced
2 garlic cloves, crushed
2.5cm/1in piece fresh root ginger, grated
5ml/1 tsp ground cumin
15ml/1 tbsp ground coriander
6 green cardamom pods
5cm/2in piece of cinnamon stick
5ml/1 tsp ground turmeric
1 fresh red chilli, seeded and finely chopped
1 potato, peeled and cut into 2.5cm/1in cubes
1 small aubergine (eggplant), halved and
    sliced or cut into chunks
115g/4oz/1½ cups mushrooms, thickly sliced
175ml/6fl oz/¾ cup water
115g/4oz/1 cup green beans, cut into
    2.5cm/1in lengths
60ml/4 tbsp natural (plain) yogurt
150ml/¼ pint/⅔ cup double (heavy) cream
5ml/1 tsp garam masala
salt and ground black pepper
fresh coriander (cilantro) sprigs, to garnish
boiled rice and poppadums, to serve

1 Melt the butter in a pan. Add the onions and cook for 5 minutes, stirring occasionally, until soft but not browned.

2 Add the garlic and ginger and cook for 2 minutes, then stir in the cumin, coriander, cardamom pods, cinnamon stick, turmeric and finely chopped chilli. Cook the spices, stirring constantly, for 30 seconds, until they are aromatic. Take care not to overcook or burn the spices as this makes them bitter.

3 Add the potato cubes, aubergine and mushrooms and the water. Cover the pan, bring to the boil, then lower the heat and simmer for 15 minutes. Add the beans and cook, uncovered, for 5 minutes. With a slotted spoon, remove the vegetables to a warmed serving dish and keep hot.

4 Increase the heat and allow the cooking liquid to bubble up until it has reduced a little. Season with salt and pepper, then stir in the yogurt, cream and garam masala. Pour the sauce over the vegetables and garnish with fresh coriander. Serve with boiled rice and crisp poppadums.

Energy 363kcal/1499kJ; Protein 4.8g; Carbohydrate 16.6g, of which sugars 8.2g; Fat 31.3g, of which saturates 19.2g; Cholesterol 78mg; Calcium 88mg; Fibre 3.7g; Sodium 104mg.

Stuffed peppers and tomatoes

Colourful peppers and tomatoes make perfect containers for stuffings. This version uses couscous with dried apricots and feta cheese. Serve with a dressed salad.

Serves four

3 ripe tomatoes
4 (bell) peppers
75g/3oz/½ cup instant couscous
75ml/2½fl oz/⅓ cup vegetable stock, boiling
15ml/1 tbsp olive oil
10ml/2 tsp white wine vinegar
50g/2oz dried apricots, finely chopped
75g/3oz feta cheese, cut into tiny cubes
45ml/3 tbsp pine nuts, toasted
30ml/2 tbsp chopped fresh parsley
salt and ground black pepper
flat leaf parsley, to garnish

1 Preheat the oven to 190°C/375°F/ Gas 5.

2 Cut the tomatoes in half and scoop out the pulp and seeds. Leave to drain on kitchen paper with cut sides down. Chop the tomato pulp and seeds.

Variation

Small aubergines (eggplants) or large courgettes (zucchini) make good vegetables for stuffing. Halve and scoop out the centres of the vegetables, then oil the vegetable cases and bake them for about 15 minutes. Chop the centres, fry for 2–3 minutes to soften and add to the stuffing mixture. Fill the cases with the stuffing and bake as for the peppers and tomatoes.

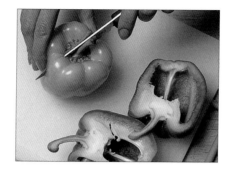

3 Halve the peppers, leaving the cores intact, and scoop out the seeds. Brush with 15ml/1 tbsp of the olive oil and bake on a baking tray for 15 minutes.

4 Place the pepper and tomato cases in a shallow ovenproof dish and season with salt and pepper.

5 Fry the onions in the remaining oil for 5 minutes. Add the garlic and chopped almonds and fry for 1 minute.

6 Remove the pan from the heat and stir in the rice, chopped tomatoes, mint, parsley and sultanas. Season well.

7 Spoon the mixture into the tomato and pepper cases. Pour 150ml/¼ pint/ ⅔ cup boiling water around the peppers and tomatoes and bake for 20 minutes.

8 Scatter with ground almonds, and sprinkle with a little extra oil. Return to the oven and bake for 20 minutes.

Energy 303kcal/1266kJ; Protein 33.7g; Carbohydrate 33.6g, of which sugars 17g; Fat 15.8g, of which saturates 3.9g; Cholesterol 113mg; Calcium 105mg; Fibre 4.3g; Sodium 285mg.

Pasta, grains and legumes

Pasta is often the first ingredient that the beginner cook turns to for an easy-to-prepare dish. It is enjoyed in soups, salads and hearty dishes, such as lasagne, or it can be dressed in a simple sauce such as a pesto. Rice, grains, peas and beans can be served as accompaniments or used to complement other ingredients. They are classic store-cupboard items, and incredibly versatile. All are available dried or in easy-cook versions, with canned legumes now more popular than their dried counterparts.

Minestrone

The classic, wintry Italian minestrone soup is made by chopping and frying vegetables, then stirring in liquid. Any small pasta shapes can be used instead of the spaghettini, if you prefer.

3 Cook the broad beans in boiling salted water for 4–5 minutes. Remove with a slotted spoon, refresh under cold water and set aside.

4 Bring the pan of water back to the boil, add the mangetouts and cook for 1 minute until just tender. Drain, then refresh under cold water and set aside.

5 Add the tomatoes and the tomato purée to the soup. Cook for 1 minute, then put two or three large ladlefuls of the soup and a quarter of the broad beans in a food processor or blender and purée until smooth. Set aside.

6 Add the spaghettini to the remaining soup and cook for 6–8 minutes, until tender. Stir in the purée and spinach and cook for 2–3 minutes. Add the rest of the broad beans, the mangetouts and parsley, and season well.

7 Stir in the basil leaves and immediately ladle the soup into deep cups or bowls. Garnish with sprigs of basil. Serve with grated Parmesan.

Serves four to six

30ml/2 tbsp olive oil
2 onions, finely chopped
2 garlic cloves, finely chopped
2 carrots, very finely chopped
1 celery stick, very finely chopped
1.3 litres/2¼ pints/5⅔ cups boiling water
450g/1lb shelled fresh broad (fava) beans
225g/8oz mangetouts (snow peas), sliced
3 tomatoes, skinned and chopped
5ml/1 tsp tomato purée (paste)
50g/2oz spaghettini, broken into
    4cm/1½in lengths
225g/8oz baby spinach
30ml/2 tbsp chopped fresh parsley
handful of fresh basil leaves
salt and ground black pepper
basil sprigs, to garnish
freshly grated Parmesan cheese, to serve

1 Heat the oil in a large pan and add the onions and garlic. Cook, stirring, for 4–5 minutes, until the onion is softened but not browned.

2 Add the carrots and celery, and cook for 2–3 minutes. Pour in the boiling water and bring to the boil. Reduce the heat and simmer for 15 minutes.

Variations
• Replace the fresh basil and Parmesan with a spoonful of pesto in each bowl of soup.
• Add bacon and borlotti beans instead of broad (fava) beans for a more hearty version.

Energy 324kcal/1356kJ; Protein 13.4g; Carbohydrate 32.3g, of which sugars 12.3g; Fat 16.6g, of which saturates 3.9g; Cholesterol 19mg; Calcium 111mg; Fibre 8.5g; Sodium 696mg.

Rigatoni with tomato sauce

Canned tomatoes combined with soffritto (the sautéed mixture of chopped onion, carrot, celery and garlic) and herbs make a sauce that is rich and full of flavour.

Serves six to eight

1 onion
1 carrot
1 celery stick
60ml/4 tbsp olive oil
1 garlic clove, thinly sliced
a few leaves each fresh basil, thyme and
    oregano or marjoram
2 x 400g/14oz cans chopped
    plum tomatoes
15ml/1 tbsp sun-dried tomato paste
5ml/1 tsp sugar
about 90ml/6 tbsp dry red or white
    wine (optional)
350g/12oz/3 cups dried rigatoni
salt and ground black pepper
coarsely shaved Parmesan cheese, to serve

3 Add the tomatoes, tomato paste and sugar, then stir in the wine, if using. Add salt and pepper to taste. Bring to the boil, stirring, then reduce the heat and simmer gently, uncovered, for about 45 minutes, stirring occasionally, until the sauce is well flavoured.

4 Cook the pasta according to the instructions on the packet. Drain and tip it into a warmed bowl. Taste the sauce for seasoning, pour the sauce over the pasta and toss well. Serve immediately, with shavings of Parmesan handed around separately. If you like, garnish with extra chopped herbs.

COOK'S TIP
Tomato sauce is a really versatile sauce to make in batches and store in the freezer. Use it as the base for a pizza topping, for serving with pasta, as the base for soup, or other vegetarian stew.

1 Chop the onion, carrot and celery finely, in a food processor or by hand.

2 Heat the olive oil in a pan, add the garlic and stir over a very low heat for 1–2 minutes. Add the chopped vegetables and herbs. Cook over a low heat, stirring frequently, for 5–7 minutes until the vegetables are soft and lightly coloured.

Variation
Add a seeded and chopped fresh green chilli with the garlic. Hard boil, shell and roughly chop 1 egg per person and sprinkle over each portion with lots of shredded basil.

Energy 313kcal/1323kJ; Protein 8.8g; Carbohydrate 51g, of which sugars 8.8g; Fat 8.6g, of which saturates 1.2g; Cholesterol 0mg; Calcium 43mg; Fibre 3.3g; Sodium 62mg.

Spaghetti with carbonara sauce

This is an all-time favourite combination of pasta coated in an egg, bacon and cream sauce.
The pancetta or bacon gives depth and the cream adds a mellow flavour.

Serves four

30ml/2 tbsp olive oil
1 small onion, finely chopped
8 rindless smoked streaky (fatty) bacon
  rashers (strips), cut into 1cm/½in strips
350g/12oz fresh or dried spaghetti
4 eggs
60ml/4 tbsp crème fraîche
60ml/4 tbsp freshly grated Parmesan cheese,
  plus extra to serve
salt and ground black pepper

1 Heat the oil in a large pan, add the onion and cook over a low heat, stirring frequently, for 5 minutes until softened but not coloured.

COOK'S TIP
Fresh pasta, if you can get it, tastes best with this dish.

2 Add the strips of bacon to the onion in the pan and cook for about 10 minutes, stirring almost all the time. Meanwhile, cook the pasta in a pan of salted boiling water according to the instructions on the packet until al dente.

3 Put the eggs, crème fraîche and grated Parmesan in a bowl. Grind in plenty of pepper, then beat everything together well.

4 Drain the pasta, tip it into the pan with the bacon and toss well to mix. Turn the heat off under the pan. Immediately add the egg mixture and toss vigorously so that it cooks lightly and coats the pasta.

5 Quickly taste for seasoning, then divide among four warmed bowls and sprinkle with black pepper. Serve immediately, with extra grated Parmesan handed separately.

Energy 708kcal/2966kj; Protein 30.7g; Carbohydrate 66.6g; of which sugars 4.2g; Fat 37.5g; of which saturates 15.5g; Cholesterol 261mg; Calcium 250mg; Fibre 2.8g; Sodium 824mg

Tuna cannelloni

There is something very appealing about cannelloni, and it is not difficult to make. The trick is to allow plenty of time because filling pasta tubes in a hurry is not a good idea.

Serves four to six

50g/2oz/¼ cup butter
50g/2oz/½ cup plain (all-purpose) flour
about 900ml/1½ pints/3¾ cups hot milk
2 x 200g/7oz cans tuna, drained
115g/4oz/1 cup Fontina cheese, grated
pinch of grated nutmeg
12 no-precook cannelloni tubes
50g/2oz/⅔ cup Parmesan cheese, grated
salt and ground black pepper
fresh herbs, to garnish

3 Gradually whisk the remaining milk into the rest of the sauce, then return the pan to the heat and simmer the sauce, whisking constantly, until the sauce is smooth. Add the grated Fontina and nutmeg, with salt and pepper to taste. Simmer for a few more minutes, stirring frequently. Pour about one-third of the sauce into a baking dish and spread to the corners.

4 Fill the cannelloni tubes with tuna mixture, pushing it in with the handle of a teaspoon. Place the cannelloni in a single layer in the dish. Thin the remaining sauce with a little more milk if necessary, then pour it over the cannelloni. Sprinkle with Parmesan cheese and bake for 30 minutes or until golden. Serve hot, garnished with herbs.

1 Melt the butter in a heavy pan, add the flour and stir over a low heat for 1–2 minutes. Remove the pan from the heat and gradually add 350ml/12fl oz/ 1½ cups of the milk, beating vigorously after each addition. Return the pan to the heat and whisk for 1–2 minutes until the sauce is very thick and smooth. Remove from the heat.

2 Mix the tuna with 120ml/4fl oz/½ cup of the white sauce in a bowl. Add salt and black pepper, to taste. Preheat the oven to 180°C/350°F/Gas 4.

Energy 502kcal/2110kJ; Protein 32.2g; Carbohydrate 44.3g, of which sugars 2.6g; Fat 22.7g, of which saturates 11.4g; Cholesterol 76mg; Calcium 293mg; Fibre 1.7g; Sodium 467mg.

Fusilli with wild mushrooms

A very rich dish with an earthy flavour and lots of garlic, this makes an ideal main course for vegetarians, especially when served with a mixed vegetable salad for colour and freshness.

Serves four

1½ x 275g/10oz jar wild mushrooms
   in olive oil
25g/1oz/2 tbsp butter
225g/8oz/2 cups fresh wild mushrooms,
   sliced if large
5ml/1 tsp finely chopped fresh thyme
5ml/1 tsp finely chopped fresh marjoram or
   oregano, plus extra herbs to serve
4 garlic cloves, crushed
350g/12oz/3 cups fresh or dried fusilli
200ml/7fl oz/scant 1 cup double
   (heavy) cream
salt and ground black pepper

1 Drain about 15ml/1 tbsp of the oil from the mushrooms into a pan. Slice or chop the bottled mushrooms into bitesize pieces, if they are large.

2 Add the butter to the oil in the pan and place over a low heat until sizzling. Add the bottled and the fresh mushrooms, the chopped herbs and the garlic, with salt and pepper to taste. Simmer over a medium heat, stirring frequently, for about 10 minutes or until the fresh mushrooms are tender.

3 Meanwhile, cook the pasta in plenty of salted, boiling water according to the instructions on the packet until tender but not soft.

4 When the mushrooms are cooked, increase the heat to high and stir and turn the mixture with a wooden spoon to evaporate any excess liquid.

5 Pour in the cream and bring to the boil, stirring, then remove from the heat at once. Taste and season if needed.

6 Drain the pasta and tip it into a warmed bowl. Pour the sauce over the pasta and toss well together. Serve immediately, sprinkled with herbs.

Energy 656kcal/2741kJ; Protein 13g; Carbohydrate 66.1g, of which sugars 4g; Fat 39.5g, of which saturates 21g; Cholesterol 82mg; Calcium 53mg; Fibre 3.6g; Sodium 56mg.

Pasta with green pesto

Rich and flavourful pesto is the perfect accompaniment to pasta. It has a sharp concentrated taste of basil and cheese. A little goes a long way, so use it sparingly.

Serves four

50g/2oz/1⅓ cups fresh basil leaves, plus a
  few fresh basil leave, to garnish
2–4 garlic cloves
60ml/4 tbsp pine nuts
120ml/4fl oz/½ cup extra virgin olive oil
115g/4oz/1⅓ cups freshly grated Parmesan
  cheese, plus extra to serve
25g/1oz/⅓ cup freshly grated
  Pecorino cheese
400g/14oz/3½ cups dried eliche
salt and ground black pepper

1 Put the basil leaves, garlic and pine nuts in a blender or food processor. Add 60ml/4 tbsp of the olive oil. Process until the ingredients are finely chopped, then stop the machine, remove the lid and scrape down the sides of the bowl.

2 Turn the machine on again and slowly pour the remaining oil in a thin, steady stream. Stop the machine and scrape down the sides of the bowl to make sure everything is evenly mixed.

3 Scrape the mixture into a large bowl and beat in the cheeses with a wooden spoon. Taste and season if necessary. Set aside while the pasta cooks, or decant into a smaller bowl to put in the refrigerator for use later (see cook's tip).

4 Cook the pasta according to the instructions on the packet. Drain it well, then add it to the bowl of pesto and toss well. Serve immediately, garnished with the fresh basil leaves and freshly grated Parmesan.

> **COOK'S TIP**
> Pesto can be made up to 2–3 days in advance. To store pesto, transfer it to a small bowl and pour a thin film of olive oil over the surface. Cover the bowl tightly with clear film (plastic wrap) and keep it in the refrigerator.

Energy 314kcal/1322kJ; Protein 15.4g; Carbohydrate 43.5g, of which sugars 3.6g; Fat 10.3g, of which saturates 3.4g; Cholesterol 14mg; Calcium 176mg; Fibre 2.7g; Sodium 216mg.

Salmon risotto

The subtle flavour of cucumber is a familiar companion for salmon. In this simple risotto fresh tarragon adds its unmistakable, delicate aroma and flavour.

Serves four

25g/1oz/2 tbsp butter
small bunch of spring onions (scallions),
    white parts only, chopped
½ cucumber, peeled, seeded
    and chopped
350g/12oz/1¾ cups risotto rice
1.2 litres/2 pints/5 cups hot chicken
    or fish stock
150ml/¼ pint/⅔ cup dry white wine
450g/1lb salmon fillet, skinned
    and diced
45ml/3 tbsp chopped fresh tarragon
salt and ground black pepper

1 Heat the butter in a pan and add the spring onions and cucumber. Cook for 2–3 minutes, stirring occasionally. Do not let the spring onions brown.

2 Stir in the risotto rice, then pour in the stock and white wine. Bring to the boil, then lower the heat and allow to simmer, uncovered, for 10 minutes, stirring occasionally. The rice should absorb most of the liquid.

3 Stir in the salmon and then season to taste. Continue cooking for a further 5 minutes, stirring occasionally to avoid sticking, then remove from the heat. Cover the pan and leave the risotto to stand for 5 minutes.

4 Remove the lid, add the chopped fresh tarragon and mix lightly, preferably with a fork. Spoon the risotto into a warmed bowl and serve immediately.

> **COOK'S TIP**
> The classic method for making risotto is to add the liquid in stages. The standing time at the end of cooking is vital for succulent rice and fish.

Energy 597kcal/2492kJ; Protein 30.9g; Carbohydrate 67.1g, of which sugars 1.5g; Fat 19.1g, of which saturates 5.4g; Cholesterol 70mg; Calcium 59mg; Fibre 0.6g; Sodium 96mg.

Garlic rice with mushrooms

Rice is readily infused with the pungent aroma and flavour of garlic chives, creating a dish with an excellent flavour. Serve as a vegetarian supper dish or to accompany fish or chicken.

Serves four

350g/12oz/generous 1½ cups
    long grain rice
60ml/4 tbsp groundnut (peanut) oil
1 small onion, finely chopped
2 green chillies, seeded and finely chopped
25g/1oz garlic chives, chopped
15g/½oz fresh coriander (cilantro)
600ml/1 pint/2½ cups vegetable or
    mushroom stock
5ml/1 tsp salt
250g/9oz mixed mushrooms, thickly sliced
50g/2oz cashew nuts, fried in 15ml/
    1 tbsp oil until golden brown
ground black pepper

1 Wash and drain the rice. Heat half the oil in a pan and cook the onion and chillies over a gentle heat, stirring occasionally, for 10–12 minutes, until soft but not browned.

2 Set half the garlic chives aside. Cut the stalks off the coriander and set the leaves aside. Purée the remaining chives and the coriander stalks with the stock in a blender or food processor.

3 Add the rice to the onions and fry over a low heat, stirring frequently, for 4–5 minutes. Pour in the stock, then stir and season well. Bring to the boil, stir just once to make sure the rice does not stick to the pan and reduce the heat to very low. Cover tightly and cook for 15–20 minutes, until the rice has absorbed all the liquid.

4 Heat the remaining oil in a frying pan and cook the mushrooms for 5–6 minutes, until tender. Add the remaining chives and cook for 1–2 minutes.

5 When the rice is cooked, place a clean, folded dish towel over the pan under the lid and press on the lid to wedge it firmly in place.

6 Leave to stand for 10 minutes, allowing the towel to absorb the steam while the rice becomes completely tender.

7 Stir the mushrooms and chopped coriander leaves into the rice. Adjust the seasoning, transfer to a warmed serving dish and serve immediately, scattered with the cashew nuts.

Energy 535kcal/2227kJ; Protein 11g; Carbohydrate 74.7g, of which sugars 1.9g; Fat 21g, of which saturates 3g; Cholesterol 0mg; Calcium 37mg; Fibre 1.8g; Sodium 41mg.

Barley risotto

This is more like a pilaff, made with slightly chewy pearl barley, than a classic risotto. Sweet leeks and mellow roasted squash are superb with this nutty grain, which is very simple to cook. The result is a flavourful and filling supper.

3 Place the squash in a roasting pan with half the thyme. Season with pepper and toss with half the oil. Roast for 30–35 minutes, stirring once.

4 Heat half the butter with the remaining oil in a large frying pan. Add the leeks and garlic and cook gently for 5 minutes. Add the mushrooms and remaining thyme, then cook until the liquid evaporates and the mushrooms begin to fry.

Serves four to five

200g/7oz/1 cup pearl barley
1 butternut squash, peeled, seeded
   and cut into chunks
10ml/2 tsp chopped fresh thyme
60ml/4 tbsp olive oil
25g/1oz/2 tbsp butter
4 leeks, cut into fairly thick diagonal slices
2 garlic cloves, finely chopped
175g/6oz chestnut mushrooms, sliced
2 carrots, coarsely grated
about 120ml/4fl oz/½ cup vegetable stock
30ml/2 tbsp chopped fresh flat leaf parsley
50g/2oz Pecorino cheese, grated
   or shaved
45ml/3 tbsp pumpkin seeds, toasted, or
   chopped walnuts
salt and ground black pepper

1 Rinse the barley well under cold running water. Drain and then cook it in simmering water, keeping the pan part-covered, for 35–45 minutes, or until tender. Drain.

2 Preheat the oven to 200°C/400°F/ Gas 6.

5 Stir in the carrots and cook for 2 minutes, then add the barley and most of the stock. Season well and part-cover the pan. Cook for a further 5 minutes. Pour in the remaining stock if the mixture seems dry.

6 Stir in the parsley, the remaining butter and half the Pecorino. Then stir in the squash. Add seasoning to taste and serve immediately, sprinkled with the toasted pumpkin seeds or walnuts and the remaining Pecorino.

Energy 498kcal/2089kJ; Protein 15.6g; Carbohydrate 55.6g, of which sugars 11.2g; Fat 25.2g, of which saturates 5.2g; Cholesterol 13mg; Calcium 287mg; Fibre 7.6g; Sodium 156mg.

Spicy chickpea samosas

A blend of crushed chickpeas and coriander sauce makes an interesting nutty and aromatic filling in these little pastries. The samosas are delicious served with a simple dip made from Greek yogurt and chopped fresh mint leaves.

Makes eighteen

2 x 400g/14oz cans chickpeas,
   drained and rinsed
120ml/4fl oz/½ cup hara masala or
   coriander (cilantro) sauce
275g/10oz filo pastry
60ml/4 tbsp chilli and garlic oil

1 Preheat the oven to 220°C/425°F/ Gas 7.

2 Process half the chickpeas to a paste in a food processor.

3 Transfer the paste to a bowl and mix in the whole chickpeas, the hara masala or coriander sauce, and a little salt. Mix until well combined.

Variation
For a milder flavour use butter instead of oil when brushing the filo pastry.

4 Place a sheet of filo pastry on a work surface and cut into three strips. Brush the strips with a little of the oil. Place a dessertspoon of the filling at one end of a strip. Turn one corner diagonally over the filling to meet the long edge. Continue folding along the length of the strip, turning the filling and pastry and keeping the triangular shape.

5 Transfer to a baking sheet and repeat with the remaining filling and pastry.

6 Place the pastries on a baking sheet and brush with any remaining oil. Bake for 15 minutes, until the pastry is golden. Cool slightly before serving.

Energy 119kcal/499kJ; Protein 4.1g; Carbohydrate 13.7g, of which sugars 0.4g; Fat 5.7g, of which saturates 0.8g; Cholesterol 0mg; Calcium 36mg; Fibre 2.2g; Sodium 99mg.

Spiced lentil soup

A subtle blend of spices and coconut alters the taste of this classic soup. Serve with crusty bread or warm naan bread to complement the smooth, luscious flavours. The fragrant spices give a warming quality without the harshness of chillies.

Serves six

2 onions, finely chopped
2 garlic cloves, crushed
4 tomatoes, roughly chopped
pinch of ground turmeric
5ml/1 tsp ground cumin
6 cardamom pods
½ cinnamon stick
225g/8oz/1 cup red lentils
400g/14oz can coconut milk
15ml/1 tbsp fresh lime juice
salt and ground black pepper
cumin seeds, to garnish

COOK'S TIP
If the fresh tomatoes are not really ripe and lack flavour or sweetness, you can stir in a little tomato purée (paste). Alternatively, use a small can of chopped tomatoes instead.

1 Put the onions, garlic, tomatoes, turmeric, cumin, cardamom pods, cinnamon and lentils into a pan with 900ml/1½ pints/3¾ cups water. Bring to the boil, lower the heat, cover and simmer gently for 20 minutes, or until the lentils are soft.

2 Remove the cardamom pods and cinnamon stick, then purée the mixture in a food processor. Sieve (strain) the soup, then return it to a clean pan.

3 Reserve a little of the coconut milk for the garnish and add the remainder to the pan with the lime juice. Stir well, then reheat the soup gently, stirring to prevent it from sticking to the pan, and without allowing it to boil. Taste the soup and season with salt and pepper, if needed.

4 Ladle the soup into bowls and swirl in the reserved coconut milk. Garnish with cumin seeds.

Energy 235kcal/991kJ; Protein 13g; Carbohydrate 28.4g, of which sugars 3.7g; Fat 8.8g, of which saturates 2.2g; Cholesterol 0mg; Calcium 66mg; Fibre 2.9g; Sodium 40mg.

Dhal

This spicy lentil mixture, cooked in the style of Indian dhal, makes a well-balanced meal when served with basmati rice or Indian breads. If you don't like hot chillies, leave out the dried red ones, but keep in the green for their flavour. Serve hot with rice or warm breads.

Serves four

45ml/3 tbsp groundnut (peanut) oil
4–5 shallots, sliced
2 garlic cloves, thinly sliced
1 onion, chopped
2 green chillies, seeded and chopped
15ml/1 tbsp chopped fresh root ginger
225g/8oz/1 cup yellow or red lentils
900ml/1½ pints/3¾ cups water
200g/7oz tomatoes, skinned and diced
a little lemon juice
45ml/3 tbsp puréed roasted garlic
5ml/1 tsp ground cumin
5ml/1 tsp ground coriander
salt and ground black pepper
5ml/1 tsp cumin seeds
5ml/1 tsp mustard seeds
3–4 small dried red chillies
8–10 fresh curry leaves
coriander (cilantro) sprigs, to garnish

1 Heat 30ml/2 tbsp of the oil in a large, heavy pan. Fry the shallots over medium heat until crispy, then add the garlic and stir until coloured. Remove with a slotted spoon and set aside.

2 Add the onion, chillies and ginger to the oil remaining in the pan and cook for 10 minutes, until golden.

3 Stir in the lentils and add the water, then bring to the boil, reduce the heat and part-cover the pan. Simmer, stirring occasionally, for 50–60 minutes, until it is the consistency of thick soup.

4 Stir the tomatoes into the dhal and then adjust the seasoning, adding a little lemon juice to taste, if necessary.

5 Add the roasted garlic purée, cumin and ground coriander, then season with salt and pepper to taste again.

6 Cook for 10–15 minutes, stirring to stop the mixture from sticking.

7 Heat the remaining oil in a frying pan. With the pan over low to medium heat, add the cumin and mustard seeds and fry for a few seconds until the mustard seeds pop. Remove from the heat immediately before the spices burn.

8 Stir the roasted seeds into the dhal with the chillies and curry leaves. Serve, garnished with coriander and shallots.

Energy 234kcal/979kJ; Protein 9.5g; Carbohydrate 23.8g, of which sugars 3.1g; Fat 11.8g, of which saturates 5.3g; Cholesterol 20mg; Calcium 28mg; Fibre 2.5g; Sodium 73mg.

Fish and shellfish

The variety of dishes in this chapter indicates how versatile and exciting fish and shellfish are as cooking ingredients. From indulgent crisp-coated fried fish or simple grilled hake to stylish seared tuna, there are all sorts of ways to treat fresh, frozen or canned seafood. This section shows you how to make the most of these quick-to-cook foods.

Seared tuna salad Niçoise

Freshly seared tuna steaks transform this classic salad from the south of France into a special dish that makes a great supper to share with friends. Be careful not to overcook the tuna.

Serves four

4 tuna steaks, each about 150/5oz
30ml/2 tbsp olive oil
salt and ground black pepper
225g/8oz fine French beans, trimmed
2 Little Gem (Bibb) lettuces
4 new potatoes, boiled
4 ripe tomatoes or 12 cherry tomatoes
2 red (bell) peppers, seeded and sliced
4 hard-boiled eggs, sliced
8 drained anchovy fillets in oil,
    halved lengthways
16 large black olives
12 fresh basil leaves, to garnish

For the dressing

15ml/1 tbsp red wine vinegar
90ml/6 tbsp olive oil
1 fat garlic clove, crushed

1 Brush the tuna on both sides with olive oil and season well. Heat the grill (broiler) until very hot, then grill (broil) the tuna for 1–2 minutes on each side; it should be pink and juicy in the centre.

2 Cook the beans in a pan of salted boiling water for 4–5 minutes. Drain, refresh with cold water and drain again.

3 Separate the lettuce leaves and wash and dry them. Arrange them on four plates. Slice the potatoes and tomatoes, and divide them among the plates. Arrange the fine French beans and red pepper strips over them.

4 Shell the hard-boiled eggs and cut them into thick slices. Divide the eggs among the four plates and drape over a couple of anchovy fillets. Scatter four olives on each plate.

5 To make the dressing, whisk together the vinegar, olive oil and garlic and season to taste. Drizzle over the salads, arrange the tuna steaks on top, scatter over the basil leaves and serve.

> **COOK'S TIP**
> Tuna is often served pink in the middle, rare like beef. If you prefer it cooked through, reduce the heat and cook for an extra few minutes, but take care not to overcook.

Energy 578kcal/2408kJ; Protein 46.4g; Carbohydrate 15g, of which sugars 10.6g; Fat 37.5g, of which saturates 7.1g; Cholesterol 235mg; Calcium 127mg; Fibre 4.7g; Sodium 585mg.

Fish and chips

This classic dish of fish cooked in batter and served with chips is one of England's national dishes. A portion of peas goes well. Salt and vinegar are traditional accompaniments.

Serves four

115g/4oz/1 cup self-raising (self-rising) flour
salt and ground black pepper
150ml/¼ pint/⅔ cup water
675g/1½lb potatoes
oil, for deep frying
675g/1½lb skinned cod fillet, cut into
    four pieces
lemon wedges, to serve

1 Stir the flour and salt together in a bowl, then make a well in the centre. Gradually whisk in the water to make a smooth batter. Leave to rest for 30 minutes.

2 Cut the potatoes into strips about 1cm/½in wide and a similar length to each other so that they cook evenly. Put the potato chips in a colander and rinse them under cold running water. Dry well.

3 Heat the oil in a deep-fat fryer or large heavy pan to 150°C/300°F. Don't leave the pan unattended.

4 Using a wire basket, lower the potatoes in batches into the hot oil and cook for 5–6 minutes, shaking the basket occasionally until the chips are soft but not browned. Remove the chips from the oil and drain them thoroughly on kitchen paper.

5 Increase the heat of the oil in the fryer to 190°C/375°F. Season the pieces of fish with salt and pepper. Stir the batter, then dip the fish into it, one piece at a time, allowing the excess to drain off.

6 Working in two batches if necessary, lower the fish into the hot oil and fry for 6–8 minutes, until crisp and brown. Drain the fish on kitchen paper and keep warm.

7 Make sure the oil is hot again, then add a batch of chips, cooking for 2–3 minutes, until brown and crisp. Keep hot while cooking the other batches. Sprinkle with salt and vinegar to serve.

Energy 645kcal/2700kJ; Protein 32.6.4g; Carbohydrate 54.3g, of which sugars 0.7g; Fat 34.5g, of which saturates 3.5g; Cholesterol 38mg; Calcium 130mg; Fibre 3.4g; Sodium 294mg.

Grilled hake with lemon and chilli

Choose firm hake fillets, as thick as possible, or try other fish, either white fish or oily fish, such as mackerel fillets or tuna steaks. The lemon and chilli also taste good with rich salmon. Serve with creamy mashed potatoes, new potatoes or on a bed of couscous.

Serves four

4 hake fillets, each weighing 150g/5oz
30ml/2 tbsp olive oil
finely grated rind and juice
   of 1 unwaxed lemon
15ml/1 tbsp crushed chilli flakes
salt and ground black pepper

COOK'S TIPS
• Cook the fish fairly near to the heat source in step 2. The flesh should be opaque and almost cooked.
• When sprinkled with lemon and chilli, the fish will burn easily, so at step 3 cook it further from the heat.

1 Preheat the grill (broiler) to high. Brush the hake fillets all over with the olive oil and place them skin side up on a baking sheet.

2 Grill (broil) the fish for 4–5 minutes, until the skin is brown and crispy, then carefully turn each fillet over using a fish slice or metal spatula.

3 Sprinkle the fillets with the lemon rind and chilli flakes and season with salt and ground black pepper.

4 Grill for a further 2–3 minutes, or until the hake is cooked through. (Test using the point of a sharp knife; the flesh should flake.) Squeeze over the lemon juice just before serving.

Energy 188kcal/786kJ; Protein 27g; Carbohydrate 0.1g, of which sugars 0.1g; Fat 8.8g, of which saturates 1.2g; Cholesterol 35mg; Calcium 22mg; Fibre 0g; Sodium 150mg.

Roast cod wrapped in prosciutto

Wrapping chunky fillets of cod in wafer-thin slices of prosciutto keeps the fish succulent and moist, at the same time adding flavour and visual impact. Serve with baby new potatoes and a herb salad for a stylish supper or lunch dish.

Serves four

2 thick skinless cod fillets, each weighing about 375g/13oz
75ml/5 tbsp extra virgin olive oil
75g/3oz prosciutto, thinly sliced
400g/14oz tomatoes, on the vine
salt and ground black pepper

1 Preheat the oven to 220°C/425°F/ Gas 7. Pat the fish dry on kitchen paper and remove any stray bones.

2 Place one fillet in an ovenproof dish and drizzle 15ml/1 tbsp of the oil over it. Cover with the second fillet, laying a thick end on top of a thin end to create an even shape.

3 Arrange the ham over the fish, overlapping the slices to cover the fish in an even layer. Tuck the ends of the ham under the fish and tie it in place at intervals with fine string.

4 Using kitchen scissors, snip the tomato vines into four portions and add these to the dish. Drizzle the tomatoes and ham with the remaining oil and season lightly. Roast for about 35 minutes, until the tomatoes are tender and lightly coloured and the fish is cooked through. Test the fish by piercing one end of the parcel with the tip of a sharp knife to check that it flakes easily.

5 Slice the fish and transfer the portions to warm plates, adding the tomatoes. Spoon over the cooking juices from the dish and serve immediately.

Energy 281kcal/1172kJ; Protein 32.8g; Carbohydrate 3.1g, of which sugars 3.1g; Fat 15.3g, of which saturates 2.3g; Cholesterol 81mg; Calcium 23mg; Fibre 1g; Sodium 116mg.

Cod gratin

This rich version of an old favourite requires minimum effort and gives maximum flavour – forget about simmering sauces and try this rich cream and cheese topping for a special treat.

3 Divide the cheese mixture among the portions of fish, spreading it over thickly and evenly. Bake for 20 minutes until browned and bubbling. The fish should be flaky and tender. Serve immediately.

Variations
• Try 90ml/6 tbsp quark or low-fat soft cheese mixed with 45ml/2 tbsp grated Parmesan cheese and 15ml/1 tbsp Dijon mustard. Add a handful of chopped fresh dill or tarragon sprigs. Spread this over the fish instead of the Cheddar.
• Mash 100g/4oz feta cheese and mix in 2 chopped spring onions (scallions) and a few chopped black olives. Grated lemon rind and a crushed garlic clove go well. Use instead of the Cheddar mix.

Serves four

4 portions of skinless cod fillet, weighing about 175g/6oz each
200g/7oz/1¾ cups mature (sharp) Cheddar cheese, finely grated
15ml/1 tbsp wholegrain mustard
75ml/5 tbsp double (heavy) cream
salt and ground black pepper

1 Preheat the oven to 200°C/400°F/ Gas 6. Check the fish for any stray bones. Grease the base and sides of an ovenproof dish, then place the fish skinned side down in the dish. Season the fish lightly with salt and pepper.

2 Mix the grated cheese and mustard together with enough cream to form a thick but spreadable paste. Ensure that the ingredients are well mixed using the back of a spoon.

Energy 445kcal/1852kJ; Protein 46g; Carbohydrate 0.4g, of which sugars 0.4g; Fat 27.7g, of which saturates 17.3g; Cholesterol 157mg; Calcium 395mg; Fibre 0g; Sodium 474mg.

Green prawn curry

A firm favourite, this prawn dish is quick and easy using just one cooking pot. This dish is mild and flavourful with a creamy taste; if you like more heat add more spice.

Serves four to six

30ml/2 tbsp vegetable oil
30ml/2 tbsp green curry paste
450g/1lb raw king prawns (jumbo shrimp), peeled and deveined
4 kaffir lime leaves, torn
1 lemon grass stalk, bruised and chopped
250ml/8fl oz/1 cup coconut milk
30ml/2 tbsp fish sauce
½ cucumber, seeded and cut into batons
10–15 basil leaves
4 fresh green chillies, sliced, to garnish

3 Stir in the coconut milk and bring to a gentle boil. Simmer, stirring occasionally, for about 5 minutes or until the prawns are tender.

4 Stir in the fish sauce, cucumber batons and whole basil leaves, then top with the green chillies and serve from the pan.

1 Heat the oil in a wok or large pan. Add the green curry paste and fry gently until bubbling and fragrant.

2 Add the prawns, kaffir lime leaves and chopped lemon grass. Fry for 2 minutes, until the prawns are pink.

Variation
Strips of chicken can be added in step 2 instead of prawns (shrimp).

Energy 115kcal/481kJ; Protein 14.1g; Carbohydrate 4g, of which sugars 2.6g; Fat 4.8g, of which saturates 0.6g; Cholesterol 146mg; Calcium 107mg; Fibre 1.3g; Sodium 567mg.

Seafood gumbo

Gumbo is a cross between a soup and stew, served over rice as a main course. Spicy sausage and seafood are key ingredients, and the combination is fabulous.

Serves four

450g/1lb fresh mussels
450g/1lb raw prawns (shrimp), in the shell
1 cooked crab, about 1kg/2¼lb
small bunch of parsley, leaves chopped and
   stalks reserved
150ml/¼ pint/⅔ cup vegetable oil
115g/4oz/1 cup plain (all-purpose) flour
1 green (bell) pepper, seeded and chopped
1 large onion, chopped
2 celery sticks, sliced
3 garlic cloves, finely chopped
75g/3oz smoked spiced sausage,
   skinned and sliced
275g/10oz/1½ cups white long grain rice
6 spring onions (scallions), shredded
cayenne pepper and salt, to taste
Tabasco sauce, to taste

1 Wash the mussels in several changes of cold water, pulling away the black 'beards'. Discard any that are broken or do not close when you tap them firmly.

COOK'S TIPS
• It is vital to stir constantly to darken the roux without burning. Should black specks occur at any stage of cooking, discard the roux and start again.
• Have the onion, green (bell) pepper and celery ready to add to the roux the minute it reaches the correct golden-brown stage, as this arrests its darkening.

2 Bring 250ml/8fl oz/1 cup water to the boil in a deep pan. Add the mussels, cover the pan tightly and cook over a high heat, shaking frequently, for 3 minutes. As the mussels open, lift them out with tongs into a sieve (strainer) set over a bowl. Discard any that fail to open. Shell the mussels, discarding the shells. Return the liquid from the bowl to the pan and make the quantity up to 2 litres/3½ pints/8 cups with water.

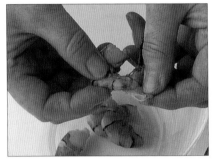

3 Peel the prawns and set them aside, reserving a few for the garnish. Put the shells and heads into the pan.

4 Remove all the meat from the crab, separating the brown and white meat. Add all the pieces of shell to the pan with 5ml/1 tsp salt.

5 Bring the stock to the boil, skimming it regularly. When there is no more froth, add the parsley stalks and simmer for 15 minutes. Cool, then strain it into a measuring jug (cup) and make up to 2 litres/3½ pints/8 cups with water.

6 Heat the oil in a heavy pan and stir in the flour. Stir constantly over a medium heat with a wooden spoon or whisk until the roux reaches a golden-brown colour. Immediately add the pepper, onion, celery and garlic. Continue cooking for about 3 minutes until the onion is soft. Stir in the sausage. Reheat the stock.

7 Stir the brown crab meat into the roux, then ladle in the hot stock a little at a time, stirring constantly until it has all been smoothly incorporated. Bring to a low boil, partially cover the pan, then simmer the gumbo for 30 minutes.

8 Cook the rice in plenty of lightly salted boiling water until the grains are tender.

9 Add the prawns, mussels, white crab meat and spring onions to the gumbo. Return to the boil and season with salt if necessary, cayenne and a dash or two of Tabasco sauce. Simmer for a further minute, then add the chopped parsley leaves. Serve with hot rice.

Energy 559kcal/2336kJ; Protein 31.1g; Carbohydrate 57.6g, of which sugars 3.7g; Fat 23g, of which saturates 3.4g; Cholesterol 183mg; Calcium 145mg; Fibre 1.9g; Sodium 474mg.

Poultry

Light poultry meat is popular worldwide. There are plenty of recipes for chicken dishes for everyday meals, as well as for special or festive dinners. Poultry is a versatile and economical food and it can be cooked in a wide variety of ways, from quick and easy ideas to more sophisticated dishes for a dinner party.

Cream of chicken soup

A rich and flavoursome creamy chicken soup makes a fabulous lunch served with crispy bread. Use decent chicken stock for this recipe to give the soup a full flavour – if you have the leftovers of a roast chicken, this is an ideal recipe for making the most of every last bit.

2 Add the stock and bring to the boil. Reduce the heat, cover the pan and simmer for 30 minutes.

3 Purée the soup. Return it to the pan. Blend the milk into the flour and stir into the soup. Bring to the boil, stirring.

4 Chop the chicken finely. Add to the soup and simmer for 5 minutes. Taste and add seasoning. Stir in half the cream and heat briefly without boiling.

5 Serve with a swirl of cream, black pepper and parsley leaves.

COOK'S TIPS
• To improve the flavour of home-made chicken soup use freshly made or defrosted frozen stock rather than that made with stock cubes.
• Use milk in place of single (light) cream, for a lower-fat dish.

Serves six

50g/2oz/¼ cup butter
2 onions, chopped
2 medium potatoes, chopped
1 large carrot, diced
1 celery stick, diced
750ml/1¼ pints/3 cups chicken stock
150ml/¼ pint/⅔ cup milk
25g/1oz/¼ cup plain (all-purpose) flour
175g/6oz cooked chicken
300ml/½ pint/1¼ cups single
   (light) cream
salt and ground black pepper
parsley leaves, to garnish

1 Melt the butter in a large pan and cook the onions, potatoes, carrot and celery for 5 minutes, stirring often, until they are soft, but do not let the vegetables brown.

Energy 295kcal/1231kJ; Protein 11g; Carbohydrate 23.6g, of which sugars 8.9g; Fat 18.2g, of which saturates 11.1g; Cholesterol 61mg; Calcium 111mg; Fibre 2.1g; Sodium 137mg.

Honey mustard chicken

This classic seasoning combination is excellent smeared on chicken portions or used to season whole chicken before roasting. Chicken thighs have a rich flavour but four chicken breast portions can be used instead. Serve with seasonal vegetables and new potatoes.

Serves four

8 chicken thighs
60ml/4 tbsp wholegrain mustard
60ml/4 tbsp clear honey
salt and ground black pepper

1 Preheat the oven to 190ºC/375ºF/ Gas 5. Put the chicken thighs in a single layer in a roasting pan.

2 Mix together the mustard and honey, season with a little salt and ground black pepper to taste. Do not add too much salt as some types of mustard are quite salty.

3 Brush the honey and mustard mixture over the chicken thighs. Roast for 25–30 minutes, basting with the pan juices occasionally, until well browned and cooked through.

Variations

Chicken with honey and mustard is brilliantly versatile as it can be served piping hot, warm or cold.
• Serve instead of a Sunday roast, with roast potatoes or boiled new or salad potatoes, buttery cabbage or broccoli and baby carrots.
• Serve hot, warm or cool on a bed of mixed salad leaves, with lots of halved cherry tomatoes and thinly sliced red onion.
• Serve instant couscous tossed with chopped chives and grated orange rind with the hot chicken. Make a salad of diced orange and diced cooked beetroot (beet) .
• Cool and chill, then pack in a container for a picnic. Take crusty bread, watercress and coleslaw.

Energy 287kcal/1205kJ; Protein 33.9g; Carbohydrate 12.1g, of which sugars 12.1g; Fat 11.8g, of which saturates 3g; Cholesterol 174mg; Calcium 30mg; Fibre 0.7g; Sodium 386mg.

Stuffed chicken wrapped with bacon

A simple cream cheese and chive filling flavours these chicken breasts and makes them deliciously moist when cooked in their bacon wrapping.

Serves four

4 skinless, boneless chicken breast portions,
    each weighing 175g/6oz
115g/4oz/½ cup cream cheese
15ml/1 tbsp chopped fresh chives
8 rindless unsmoked bacon
    rashers (strips)
15ml/1 tbsp olive oil
ground black pepper

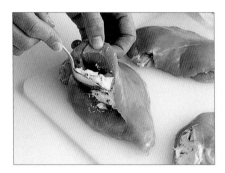 

1 Preheat the oven to 200°C/400°F/ Gas 6.

2 Using a sharp knife, make a horizontal slit into the side of each chicken portion without cutting all the way through (the filling is stuffed into each slit).

3 To make the filling, beat together the cream cheese and chives. Divide the filling into four portions and, using a teaspoon, fill each slit with a portion of the cream cheese. Press the filling in and push the sides of the slit together to keep it in place.

4 Wrap each stuffed breast in two rashers of bacon and place in an ovenproof dish. Drizzle the oil over the chicken and bake for 25–30 minutes, until lightly browned and cooked through. Season with black pepper and serve at once.

Energy 459kcal/1913kJ; Protein 52.3g; Carbohydrate 0g, of which sugars 0g; Fat 27.7g, of which saturates 13g; Cholesterol 0mg; Calcium 40mg; Fibre 0g; Sodium 1070mg.

Southern fried chicken

This simple version of fried chicken does not involve deep-frying, making it easier, less smelly and messy, and lower in fat. A good way of cooking the corn cakes is to place them in a grill pan, dot with butter and grill until golden, turning once, while frying the chicken.

Serves four

15ml/1 tbsp paprika
30ml/2 tbsp plain (all-purpose) flour
4 skinless, boneless chicken breast portions,
    each weighing 175g/6oz
30ml/2 tbsp sunflower oil
salt and ground black pepper

For the corn cakes
200g/7oz corn kernels
350g/12oz mashed potato, cooled
25g/1oz/2 tbsp butter

For the soured cream dip
150ml/¼ pint/⅔ cup soured cream
15ml/1 tbsp chopped fresh chives

1 Mix the paprika and flour together on a plate.

2 Coat each chicken portion in the seasoned flour. Heat the oil in a large frying pan and add the floured chicken. Cook over a high heat, turning once, until golden brown on both sides.

3 Reduce the heat and continue cooking for 20 minutes, turning once or twice, or until cooked through.

4 To make the corn cakes, stir the corn kernels into the cooled mashed potato and season to taste. Using lightly floured hands, shape the mixture into 12 even round cakes, each about 5cm/2in in diameter.

5 When the chicken is cooked, remove the pieces from the pan and keep hot. Melt the butter in the pan and cook the corn cakes for 3 minutes on each side, or until golden and heated through.

6 Meanwhile, mix together the soured cream with the chives in a bowl to make a dip. Transfer the corn cakes from the frying pan to serving plates and top with the chicken breast portions. Serve at once, offering the sour cream with chives on the side.

Energy 505kcal/2119kJ; Protein 47.8g; Carbohydrate 32.2g, of which sugars 3.3g; Fat 21.5g, of which saturates 9.3g; Cholesterol 158mg; Calcium 61mg; Fibre 2.5g; Sodium 172mg.

Coq au vin

This famous recipe from Burgundy, France, is a slow-cooked stew of chicken, wine, onions, bacon and mushrooms. The result is a rich and delicious dish with a depth of flavour that is perfect for Sunday lunch on a cold day. Serve with mashed potatoes and vegetables.

4 Pour in the cognac and set it alight using a long match. Remove the chicken when the flames die down.

5 Chop the remaining onions and fry them in 15g/½oz/1 tbsp butter with the garlic until softened. Preheat the oven to 160°C/325°F/Gas 3.

6 Add the wine and stock with the bouquet garni and stir in the tomato purée. Lower the heat, then simmer for 20 minutes. Stir and season.

7 Put the chicken and bacon in a flameproof casserole. Pour over the sauce. Cover and put in the oven for 1½ hours. Add the browned onions and cook for a further 30 minutes.

8 Fry the mushrooms in another 15g/½oz/1 tbsp butter and the remaining oil. Set aside. Mix the remaining butter and flour to make a paste.

9 Using a slotted spoon, transfer the chicken and onions to a serving plate. Discard the bouquet garni. Heat the cooking juices on the stove until simmering. Add the butter and flour paste in small lumps, whisking to blend the paste into the sauce as it melts. Continue until the sauce is thickened.

10 Add the mushrooms and cook for a few minutes. Pour over the chicken.

Serves four

1 bouquet garni
1 bottle full-bodied red wine
600ml/1 pint/2½ cups chicken stock
50g/2oz/4 tbsp butter
30ml/2 tbsp olive oil
24 small pickling onions
115g/4oz bacon, cut into small pieces
45ml/3 tbsp plain (all-purpose) flour
8 chicken portions
45ml/3 tbsp cognac
2 garlic cloves, chopped
15ml/1 tbsp tomato purée (paste)
250g/9oz button (white) mushrooms
30ml/2 tbsp chopped fresh parsley
salt and ground black pepper

1 Put the bouquet garnet in a large pan with the wine and stock and simmer, uncovered, for 15 minutes. Set aside to cool.

2 Melt 15g/½oz/1 tbsp of the butter with half the olive oil in a frying pan and brown 16 of the onions. Transfer the onions to a plate. Add the bacon and cook until browned, then set aside.

3 Season 30ml/2 tbsp of the flour with salt and pepper. Dust the chicken joints in the flour and fry them in the fat remaining in the pan over a medium heat, turning frequently, for 10 minutes.

Energy 630kcal/2618kJ; Protein 42.8g; Carbohydrate 19.3g, of which sugars 7.4g; Fat 41g, of which saturates 17.3g; Cholesterol 209mg; Calcium 67mg; Fibre 2.6g; Sodium 480mg.

Crème fraîche and coriander chicken

The coriander leaves have a wonderfully fresh fragrant flavour, so don't be afraid to use them generously; flat leaf parsley could also be substituted. Boneless thighs are used in this recipe, but chicken breast fillets would work equally well.

Serves four

6 skinless chicken thigh fillets
15ml/1 tbsp sunflower oil
60ml/4 tbsp crème fraîche
1 small bunch of fresh coriander (cilantro), roughly chopped
salt and ground black pepper

COOK'S TIPS

• You could use any cut of chicken to make this recipe, although thigh meat is the most flavourful.

• Serve with a jacket potato and green herb salad.

1 Cut each boneless chicken thigh into three or four pieces using a sharp knife. Heat the oil in a large frying pan, then add the chicken and cook for about 6 minutes, turning occasionally, until golden brown and cooked through.

2 Add the crème fraîche to the pan and stir until melted, then allow to bubble for 1–2 minutes.

3 Add the chopped coriander and stir to combine. Season to taste, and serve.

Energy 249kcal/1041kJ; Protein 32.1g; Carbohydrate 0.7g, of which sugars 0.6g; Fat 13.1g, of which saturates 5.6g; Cholesterol 174mg; Calcium 44mg; Fibre 0.6g; Sodium 143mg.

Duck and sesame stir-fry

For a special-occasion stir-fried duck dish, breast fillets are ideal, and can be bought boned, with skin and fat removed. Any poultry or lean diced pork or lamb can be used instead of the duck to make a more economical everyday meal.

Serves four

250g/9oz skinless boneless duck breast
15ml/1 tbsp sesame oil
15ml/1 tbsp vegetable or sunflower oil
4 garlic cloves, finely sliced
2.5ml/½ tsp dried chilli flakes
15ml/1 tbsp Thai fish sauce
15ml/1 tbsp light soy sauce
about 225g/8oz broccoli, cut into small florets
coriander (cilantro) and 15ml/1 tbsp toasted
    sesame seeds, to garnish

Variation
Replace the Thai fish sauce with the same quantity of soy sauce.

1 Cut the duck meat into bitesize pieces. Heat the oils in a wok and stir-fry the garlic over a medium heat until it is golden brown – do not let it burn. Add the duck to the pan and stir-fry for a further 2 minutes until the meat is just cooked and begins to brown.

2 Stir in the chilli flakes, fish sauce, soy sauce and 120ml/4fl oz/½ cup water. Add the broccoli and continue to stir-fry for about 2 minutes, until the duck is just cooked through. Serve on warmed plates, garnished with coriander and sesame seeds.

Energy 192kcal/798kJ; Protein 18.7g; Carbohydrate 2.7g, of which sugars 2.3g; Fat 12.9g, of which saturates 2.1g; Cholesterol 69mg; Calcium 104mg; Fibre 3.6g; Sodium 436mg.

Turkey lasagne

This easy meal-in-one pasta bake is delicious with cooked turkey and broccoli in a rich, creamy Parmesan sauce. When shopping for cookware, do not be tempted by shallow lasagne dishes; a deep dish is essential for retaining bubbling hot layers without spills in the oven.

Serves four

30ml/2 tbsp light olive oil
1 onion, chopped
2 garlic cloves, chopped
450g/1lb cooked turkey meat, finely diced
225g/8oz/1 cup mascarpone
30ml/2 tbsp chopped fresh tarragon
300g/11oz broccoli, broken into florets
115g/4oz no pre-cook lasagne verdi

For the sauce
50g/2oz/¼ cup butter
30ml/2 tbsp plain (all purpose) flour
600ml/1 pint/2½ cups milk
75g/3oz/1 cup freshly grated
    Parmesan cheese
salt and ground black pepper

1 Preheat the oven to 180°C/350°F/ Gas 4. Heat the oil in a pan and cook the onion and garlic until soft but not brown. Remove from the heat and stir in the turkey, mascarpone and tarragon, with seasoning to taste.

2 Bring a pan of salted boiling water to the boil. Add the broccoli for 1 minute to blanch, then drain and rinse under cold water to prevent the broccoli from overcooking. Drain well and set aside.

Variation
Use cauliflower florets in place of broccoli, if you prefer.

3 To make the sauce, melt the butter in a pan, stir in the flour and cook for 1 minute, still stirring. Remove from the heat and gradually stir in the milk. Return to the heat and bring to the boil, stirring constantly. Simmer for 1 minute, then add 50g/2oz/⅔ cup of the Parmesan and plenty of seasoning.

4 Spoon a layer of the turkey mixture into a large baking dish. Add a layer of broccoli and cover with sheets of lasagne. Coat with cheese sauce. Repeat these layers, finishing with a layer of cheese sauce on top. Sprinkle with the remaining Parmesan and bake for 35–40 minutes.

Energy 732kcal/3072kJ; Protein 61.6g; Carbohydrate 43g, of which sugars 13.1g; Fat 36.2g, of which saturates 19.4g; Cholesterol 138mg; Calcium 539mg; Fibre 3.6g; Sodium 475mg.

Meat

Beef, lamb and pork are the basis for all sorts of
different meals, from the most modest stewpot with
little more than a meaty bone and humble vegetables,
or a mouth-watering burger, to steaks and succulent
roasts of banqueting proportions. Many people are
fearful of cooking with meat, but there really is no
need to be concerned; all the main techniques are
fully explained in this chapter.

Beef cooked in red wine

Shin of beef is a tough cut of meat that needs long, slow cooking to make it tender and bring out the flavour, but the result is worth the wait. Marinating the beef in red wine gives a tender, full-flavoured result. Sprinkle the stew with rosemary and serve with mashed potatoes.

Serves four

675g/1½lb boneless shin or leg (shank) of
  beef, cut into cubes
3 large garlic cloves, finely chopped
1 bottle fruity red wine
salt and ground black pepper
handful of rosemary sprigs, to garnish

COOK'S TIP
This beef stew freezes well for up to 2 months. Cool the mixture, then pour into a freezer container. Push all the cubes of meat down into the sauce to prevent them drying out, cover and freeze.

1 Put the beef in a casserole dish with the garlic and some ground black pepper, and pour over the red wine. Stir to combine thoroughly, then cover and chill for at least 12 hours. This will allow the wine to flavour and tenderize the meat as it slowly marinates.

2 Preheat the oven to 160°C/325°F/ Gas 3. Cover the casserole with a tight-fitting lid and transfer to the oven. Cook for 3–3½ hours, or until the beef is tender. Season to taste, and serve, garnished with rosemary sprigs.

Variation
Add bacon and vegetables for a stew to serve six. Drain the meat (reserving the garlic and wine) and brown it. Add a chopped onion, 1 diced celery stick, 1 diced carrot with 2 diced bacon rashers (strips) with 2 bay leaves. Pour in the wine, then cook as in the main recipe.

Energy 287kcal/1196kJ; Protein 26.1g; Carbohydrate 1.1g, of which sugars 0.3g; Fat 10.5g, of which saturates 4.3g; Cholesterol 65mg; Calcium 15mg; Fibre 0.2g; Sodium 81mg.

Chilli con carne

Originally made with finely chopped beef, chillies and kidney beans by hungry labourers working on the Texan railroad, this famous Tex-Mex stew has become an international favourite. Serve with rice or baked potatoes to complete this hearty meal.

Serves eight

1.2kg/2½lb lean braising steak
30ml/2 tbsp sunflower oil
1 large onion, chopped
2 garlic cloves, finely chopped
15ml/1 tbsp plain (all-purpose) flour
300ml/½ pint/1¼ cups red wine
300ml/½ pint/1¼ cups beef stock
30ml/2 tbsp tomato purée (paste)
fresh coriander (cilantro) leaves, to garnish
salt and ground black pepper

For the beans
30ml/2 tbsp olive oil
1 onion, chopped
1 red chilli, seeded and chopped
2 x 400g/14oz cans red kidney beans,
   drained and rinsed
400g/14oz can chopped tomatoes

For the topping
6 tomatoes, peeled and chopped
1 green chilli, seeded and chopped
30ml/2 tbsp chopped fresh chives
30ml/2 tbsp chopped fresh coriander (cilantro)

1 Cut the meat into thick strips and then into small cubes.

2 Heat the oil in a flameproof casserole. Add the onion and garlic, and cook until softened but not coloured.

3 Meanwhile, heap the flour on a small plate, and season it well. Toss a batch of meat in it.

4 Use a slotted spoon to remove the onion from the pan, then add the floured beef and cook over a high heat until browned on all sides. Remove from the pan and set aside, then flour and brown another batch of meat.

5 When the last batch of meat is browned, return the first batches with the onion to the pan. Stir in the wine, stock and tomato purée. Bring to the boil, reduce the heat and simmer for 45 minutes, or until tender.

6 Meanwhile, for the beans, heat the olive oil in a frying pan and gently cook the onion and chilli until softened, about 10 minutes. Add the kidney beans and tomatoes and simmer gently for 20–25 minutes, or until thickened and reduced.

7 Mix the tomatoes, chilli, chives and coriander for the topping. Ladle the meat mixture on to warmed plates. Add a layer of bean mixture and tomato topping. Garnish with coriander.

Energy 469kcal/1963kJ; Protein 42g; Carbohydrate 28.3g, of which sugars 11.2g; Fat 18.8g, of which saturates 6.8g; Cholesterol 106mg; Calcium 127mg; Fibre 8.1g; Sodium 523mg.

All-in-one beef hot-pot

This heart-warming, rich pot-roast is ideal for a winter supper. Brisket of beef has the best flavour but this dish works equally well with rolled silverside or topside.

Serves eight

30ml/2 tbsp vegetable oil
900g/2lb rolled brisket of beef
275g/10oz onions, roughly chopped
2 celery sticks, thickly sliced
450g/1lb carrots, cut into large chunks
675g/1½lb potatoes, peeled and cut
  into large chunks
30ml/2 tbsp plain (all-purpose) flour
475ml/16fl oz/2 cups beef stock
300ml/½ pint/1¼ cups Guinness
1 bay leaf
45ml/3 tbsp chopped fresh thyme
5ml/1 tsp soft light brown sugar
30ml/2 tbsp wholegrain mustard
15ml/1 tbsp tomato purée (paste)
salt and ground black pepper

1 Preheat the oven to 180°C/350°F/ Gas 4.

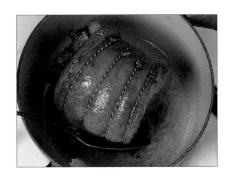

2 Heat the oil in a large, deep flameproof casserole and fry the meat until well browned on all sides. Use tongs to turn the meat.

3 Remove the meat from the pan and drain it on a double layer of kitchen paper. Add the chopped onions to the pan and cook for about 4 minutes, or until they are just beginning to soften and turn brown, stirring all the time.

4 Add the celery, carrots and potatoes to the casserole and cook over a medium heat for 2–3 minutes, or until they are just beginning to colour.

5 Stir in the flour and cook for a further 1 minute, stirring constantly. Pour in the beef stock and the Guinness and stir until well combined. Bring the sauce to the boil, stirring constantly with a wooden spoon.

6 Add the bay leaf, thyme, sugar, mustard, tomato purée and plenty of seasoning. Place the meat on top, cover tightly and transfer to the oven.

7 Cook for about 2½ hours, or until tender. Adjust the seasoning and add another pinch of sugar, if necessary.

Energy 402kcal/1691kJ; Protein 35.5g; Carbohydrate 33.8g, of which sugars 11.9g; Fat 13.6g, of which saturates 4.4g; Cholesterol 81mg; Calcium 58mg; Fibre 4g; Sodium 142mg.

Beef stroganoff

This classic recipe uses expensive fillet for a treat to share with friends. Try tender pork strips or lamb for an economical alternative. Serve with rice and a huge, leafy, herby salad on the side.

Serves eight

1.2kg/2½lb fillet of beef
30ml/2 tbsp plain (all-purpose) flour
large pinch each of cayene pepper
   and paprika
75ml/5 tbsp sunflower oil
1 large onion, chopped
3 garlic cloves, finely chopped
450g/1lb/6½ cups chestnut
   mushrooms, sliced
75ml/5 tbsp brandy
300ml/½ pint/1¼ cups beef stock
300ml/½ pint/1¼ cups soured cream
45ml/3 tbsp chopped flat leaf parsley
salt and ground black pepper

1 Thinly slice the fillet of beef across the grain, then cut it into fine strips. Season the flour with the cayenne pepper and paprika.

2 Heat half the oil in a large frying pan, add the onion and garlic and cook gently until the onion has softened.

3 Add the mushrooms and stir-fry over a high heat. Transfer the vegetables and their juices to a dish; set aside.

COOK'S TIP

If you do not have a very large pan, divide all the ingredients in half and use two pans. Alternatively, use a large flameproof casserole or even a heavy roasting pan.

4 Wipe the pan, then add and heat the remaining oil. Coat a batch of meat with flour, then stir-fry over a high heat until browned. Remove from the pan, then coat and stir-fry another batch. When the last batch of steak is cooked, replace the meat and vegetables. Add the brandy and simmer until it has almost evaporated.

5 Stir in the stock and seasoning and cook for 10–15 minutes, stirring frequently, or until the meat is tender and the sauce is thick and glossy. Add the soured cream, sprinkle with chopped parsley and remove from the heat immediately before the cream curdles. Serve at once with rice and a herby salad.

Energy 919kcal/3810kJ; Protein 32.5g; Carbohydrate 36g, of which sugars 11.7g; Fat 72.6g, of which saturates 34.6g; Cholesterol 194mg; Calcium 94mg; Fibre 3.4g; Sodium 177mg.

Three ways with fried steak

Melt-in-the-mouth fast-fried steak is often an occasional treat. Serve it with a choice of two rich sauces, or a coating of cracked peppercorns, fries and seasonal vegetables.

Serves two

2 rump, sirloin or fillet steaks,5cm/2in thick
25g/1oz butter

1 Trim any excess fat from the steaks, then season both sides.

2 Melt the butter in a frying pan and cook the steaks for about 3 minutes on each side for medium rare. Cook for a little longer if you like your steak well cooked.

MUSHROOM SAUCE

A creamy sauce densely packed with sliced mushrooms makes a delightful addition to a well-cooked steak. Garlic adds piquant flavour notes.

115g/4oz mushrooms, cleaned and chopped
1 clove garlic
15ml/1 tbsp oil
15g/½oz oil
50g/2oz butter
30ml/2 tbsp plain (all-purpose) flour
600ml/1 pint/2½ cups milk

1 Fry the mushrooms and garlic in the oil over a medium heat until softened.

2 In another pan, melt the butter. Add the flour and cook for 1 minute, stirring constantly. Turn off the heat and add the milk. Return to the heat and bring to the boil. Simmer gently for 1 minute and season. Stir in the mushrooms and mix well to combine.

STEAK AU POIVRE

A coating of cracked peppercorns adds heat to a fried steak that is not for the faint-hearted.

30–45ml/2–3 tbsp black peppercorns

1 In a mortar and using a pestle, coarsely crush the black peppercorns.

2 Tip the crushed peppercorns on to a plate and press each side of the steak into them.

3 Cook the steak as in step 2 described in column 1.

BEARNAISE SAUCE

A tangy, but rich and creamy sauce.

90ml/6 tbsp white wine vinegar
12 black peppercorns
2 bay leaves
sprig of tarragon
2 shallots, finely chopped
4 egg yolks
salt and ground black pepper
225g/8oz/1 cup unsalted (sweet) butter

1 Put the first five ingredients in a small pan and simmer until reduced to 30ml/2 tbsp of liquid when strained through a sieve (strainer).

2 In a heatproof bowl set over a pan of gently simmering water, beat 4 egg yolks. Season. Beat in the strained vinegar liquid, then add 225g/8oz/ 1 cup unsalted butter, which has been cut into cubes, one cube at a time. Serve with the steak.

Fried steak with mushroom sauce Energy 826kcal/3434kJ; Protein 46.4g; Carbohydrate 23.4g, of which sugars 15.3g; Fat 61.8g, of which saturates 33.9g; Cholesterol 208mg; Calcium 392mg; Fibre 1.1g; Sodium 602mg. Au poivre Energy 263kcal/1095kJ; Protein 34.3g; Carbohydrate 0g, of which sugars 0g; Fat 14.1g, of which saturates 5.7g; Cholesterol 87mg; Calcium 19mg; Fibre 0g; Sodium 97mg. Bearnaise sauce Energy 1218kcal/5029kJ; Protein 40.6g; Carbohydrate 1g, of which sugars 0.7g; Fat 116.9g, of which saturates 69.6g; Cholesterol 749mg; Calcium 75mg; Fibre 0.2g; Sodium 958mg.

Spaghetti with meatballs

Meatballs simmered in a sweet and spicy tomato sauce are truly delicious with spaghetti or with other pasta. Children love them and to make the dish milder you can easily leave out the chillies. This is a filling, nutritious and economic dish to cook for a midweek supper.

Serves six to eight

350g/12oz minced (ground) beef
1 egg
60ml/4 tbsp flat leaf parsley, chopped
pinch of crushed dried red chillies
1 thick slice white bread, crusts removed
30ml/2 tbsp milk
about 30ml/2 tbsp olive oil
300ml/½ pint/1¼ cups passata (bottled
    strained tomatoes)
400ml/14fl oz/1¾ cups vegetable stock
5ml/1 tsp sugar
350–450g/12oz–1lb fresh or
    dried spaghetti
salt and ground black pepper
freshly grated Parmesan cheese, to serve

1 Put the minced beef in a large bowl. Add the egg, half the parsley and half the crushed chillies. Season well.

2 Tear the bread into small pieces and place in a bowl. Moisten with the milk. Leave to soak for a few minutes, then squeeze out the excess milk and crumble the bread over the meat.

3 Mix everything together with a wooden spoon, then use your hands to squeeze and knead the mixture so that it becomes smooth and quite sticky.

4 Rinse your hands under the cold tap, shake off the excess water, then pick up small pieces and roll the mixture between your palms to make 40–60 small balls. Place the meatballs on a tray and chill for about 30 minutes.

5 Heat the oil in a frying pan. Cook the meatballs until browned on all sides.

6 Pour the passata and stock into a large pan. Heat gently, then add the remaining chillies and the sugar. Season to taste. Add the meatballs, then bring to the boil. Lower the heat, cover and simmer for 20 minutes.

7 Cook the pasta according to the packet instructions. When it is al dente, drain and tip it into a warmed large bowl. Pour the sauce over the pasta and toss gently together. Sprinkle with the remaining parsley and serve with grated Parmesan handed around separately.

> **COOK'S TIP**
> Some recipes suggest dusting hands with flour to shape meat, but the flour gets messy and sticky. Instead, keep your hands wet, which means setting up near the sink and rinsing your hands frequently under cold running water. Works every time!

Energy 324kcal/1364kJ; Protein 17.1g; Carbohydrate 40.3g, of which sugars 7.7g; Fat 11.6g, of which saturates 3.8g; Cholesterol 50mg; Calcium 51mg; Fibre 2.7g; Sodium 156mg.

Cottage pie

This classic pie is so good that it is difficult to know when second or third helpings are enough.
Serve with colourful vegetables. The meaty sauce can also be served with rice or pasta, rolled
in wheat tortillas or pancakes and topped with grated cheese, or spooned into baked potatoes.

Serves four

30ml/2 tbsp sunflower oil
1 onion, finely chopped
1 carrot, finely chopped
115g/4oz mushrooms, chopped
500g/1¼lb minced (ground) beef
300ml/½ pint/1¼ cups beef stock or water
15ml/1 tbsp plain (all-purpose) flour
1 bay leaf
10–15ml/2–3 tsp Worcestershire sauce
15ml/1 tbsp tomato purée (paste)
675g/1½lb potatoes, peeled and
   cut in chunks
25g/1oz/2 tbsp butter
45ml/3 tbsp hot milk
15ml/1 tbsp chopped fresh tarragon
salt and ground black pepper

1 Heat the oil in a pan, add the onion,
carrot and mushrooms and cook,
stirring occasionally, until browned.
Add the minced beef to the pan and
cook, stirring to break up the lumps,
until lightly browned.

2 Blend a few spoonfuls of the stock or
water with the flour, then stir this into
the pan. Stir in the remaining stock or
water and bring to a simmer, stirring.

3 Add the bay leaf, Worcestershire
sauce and tomato purée, then cover
and cook very gently for 1 hour, stirring
occasionally. Uncover the pan towards
the end of cooking to allow any excess
water to evaporate.

4 Preheat the oven to 190°C/375°F/
Gas 5. Place the potatoes in a pan with
boiling water. Boil, reduce the heat a
little and cover. Cook until soft
(15 minutes). Drain. Return to the pan.
Mash with butter, milk and seasoning.

5 Add the tarragon and seasoning to
the mince, then pour into a pie dish.
Cover the mince with an even layer of
potato and mark the top with the
prongs of a fork. Bake for about
25 minutes, until golden brown.

Energy 426kcal/1788kJ; Protein 33.9g; Carbohydrate 39.2g, of which sugars 6.3g; Fat 15.9g, of which saturates 5.9g; Cholesterol 0mg; Calcium 66mg; Fibre 3.7g; Sodium 240mg.

Chunky burgers

Burgers are easy to make and these taste terrific – far better than any you can buy. Use lean minced beef so that the burgers are not fatty. Serve in a bread bun with salad and fries.

2 To make the spicy relish, heat the olive oil in a frying pan and cook the shallot, garlic and chilli for a few minutes, stirring, until softened. Stir in the ratatouille and simmer for 5 minutes.

3 Preheat the grill (broiler) or a frying pan. Cook the burgers for 5 minutes on each side, or until cooked through.

4 Split the burger buns and toast them, if you like. Arrange a few lettuce leaves on the bun bases, then top with the burgers and add a little of the warm spicy relish. Add the bun tops and serve at once, offering the remaining relish and any extra lettuce leaves separately.

Serves four

450g/1lb lean minced (ground) beef
1 shallot, chopped
30ml/2 tbsp chopped fresh flat leaf parsley
30ml/2 tbsp tomato ketchup
salt and ground black pepper
4 burger buns, to serve
1 Little Gem (Bibb) lettuce heart, separated
  into leaves, to serve

For the spicy relish
15ml/1 tbsp olive oil
1 shallot, chopped
1 garlic clove, crushed
1 small green chilli, seeded and
  finely chopped
400g/14oz can ratatouille

1 Mix the beef, shallot, parsley, ketchup and seasoning in a mixing bowl until thoroughly combined. Divide into four portions. Shape into balls, then flatten into patties. Press the meat firmly between the palms of your hands. To prevent meat from sticking, rinse your hands under cold running water.

Variations
• For an Asian twist, add 5ml/1 tsp anchovy paste, 10ml/2 tsp ground coriander, 1 tsp ground cumin, 7.5ml/1½ tsp finely grated root ginger and two crushed garlic cloves. Serve with fresh coriander (cilantro) and mango chutney.
• Put a cube of mozzarella or blue cheese, such as Gorgonzola or Stilton in the centre for a delicious melting burger.
• Serve with chunky chips (French fries) and sour cream. A fresh green salad with spring onions (scallions) makes a good accompaniment.

Energy 484kcal/2021kJ; Protein 27.9g; Carbohydrate 30.2g, of which sugars 7.7g; Fat 28.8g, of which saturates 9.3g; Cholesterol 68mg; Calcium 120mg; Fibre 2.2g; Sodium 473mg.

Corned beef and egg hash

This is comfort food at its best! Whether you remember gran's version, or prefer this American-style hash, it turns corned beef into a supper fit for any guest.

Serves four

30ml/2 tbsp vegetable oil
25g/1oz/2 tbsp butter
1 onion, finely chopped
1 green (bell) pepper, seeded and diced
2 large potatoes, boiled and diced
350g/12oz can corned beef, cubed
pinch of grated nutmeg
pinch of paprika
4 eggs
salt and ground black pepper
parsley, to garnish (optional)
sweet chilli sauce or tomato sauce, to serve

COOK'S TIP
Put the can of corned beef into the refrigerator to chill for about half an hour before using – it will firm up and cut into cubes more easily. Buy good quality corned beef for the best flavour.

---

1 Heat the oil and butter together in a large frying pan. Add the onion and fry for 5–6 minutes until softened.

2 In a bowl, mix together the green pepper, potatoes, corned beef, nutmeg and paprika and season well. Add to the pan and toss gently to distribute the cooked onion. Press down lightly and fry without stirring on a medium heat for about 3–4 minutes until a golden brown crust has formed on the underside.

3 Stir the mixture through to distribute the crust, then repeat the frying twice, until the mixture is well browned.

4 Make four wells in the hash and carefully crack an egg into each. Cover and cook gently for about 4–5 minutes until the egg whites are set.

5 Sprinkle with parsley, if using, and cut into quarters. Serve the hash piping hot with sweet chilli sauce or a tomato sauce.

Energy 421kcal/1758kJ; Protein 30.9g; Carbohydrate 17g, of which sugars 5.4g; Fat 26.2g, of which saturates 10.6g; Cholesterol 277mg; Calcium 65mg; Fibre 1.7g; Sodium 871mg.

Lamb chops with a mint jelly crust

Mint and lamb are classic partners, and the breadcrumbs used here add extra texture. Serve the chops with sweet potatoes baked in their skins and some steamed green vegetables.

Serves four

8 lamb chops, about 115g/4oz each
50g/2oz/1 cup fresh white breadcrumbs
30ml/2 tbsp mint jelly
salt and ground black pepper

1 Preheat the oven to 190°C/375°F/Gas 5.

2 Lightly grease a baking sheet to stop the meat from sticking, then place the lamb chops on the baking sheet and season with plenty of salt and ground black pepper.

3 Put the breadcrumbs and mint jelly in a bowl and mix together to combine. The mint jelly should be at room temperature to mix well. If it has been chilled, dip the teaspoon in a cup of boiling water and this will warm the jelly.

4 Spoon the breadcrumb mixture on top of the chops, pressing down firmly with the back of a spoon, making sure it sticks to the chops. Bake the chops for 20–30 minutes, or until they are just cooked through. Serve immediately.

Energy 551kcal/2309kJ; Protein 64.1g; Carbohydrate 11.3g, of which sugars 2g; Fat 27.9g, of which saturates 13.3g; Cholesterol 248mg; Calcium 46mg; Fibre 0.3g; Sodium 316mg.

Rosemary scented lamb

The marriage of rosemary and lamb is made in heaven. This simple dish is quick to cook and prepare. Ask your butcher to 'French trim' the lamb racks.

Serves four to eight

2 x 8-chop racks of lamb
8 large fresh rosemary sprigs
2 garlic cloves, thinly sliced
90ml/6 tbsp extra virgin olive oil
30ml/2 tbsp red wine
salt and ground black pepper

1 Cut the fat off the ribs down the top 5cm/2in from the bone ends. Turn over and score between the bones.

2 Cut and scrape away the meat and connective tissue between the bones. Cut the racks into eight portions, each consisting of two linked chops, and tie a rosemary sprig to each one.

3 Arrange the portions in a single layer in a bowl or wide dish. Mix the garlic, olive oil and wine together, and pour over the lamb. Cover and chill overnight if you can, turning them as often as possible.

4 Bring the marinating chops to room temperature 1 hour before cooking. Remove the lamb from the marinade, and discard the marinade. Season the meat 15 minutes before cooking.

5 Heat the grill (broiler) to high and grill (broil) on each side for 4 minutes, if you like rare meat, or 5 minutes each side if you prefer the lamb medium-cooked.

6 Remove the chops from the grill, transfer to serving plates, cover and rest for 5–10 minutes before serving.

COOK'S TIP
Allowing the hot chops to stand before serving gives the juices time to gather and create a light sauce in much the same way that a joint needs to rest before carving.

Energy 433Kcal/1788kJ; Protein 23.4g; Carbohydrate 0g, of which sugars 0g; Fat 37.6g, of which saturates 16.4g; Cholesterol 101mg; Calcium 17mg; Fibre 0g; Sodium 83mg.

Lamb's liver with bacon casserole

The trick when cooking liver is to seal it quickly in a hot pan, then simmer it briefly and gently. Prolonged and/or fierce cooking makes the liver hard and grainy, which needs to be avoided. Boiled new potatoes tossed in lots of butter go well with this simple casserole.

Serves four

30ml/2 tbsp extra virgin olive oil or
  sunflower oil
225g/8oz rindless unsmoked lean bacon
  rashers (strips), cut into pieces
2 onions, halved and sliced
175g/6oz/2 cups chestnut
  mushrooms, halved
450g/1lb lamb's liver, trimmed
  and sliced
25g/1oz/2 tbsp butter
15ml/1 tbsp soy sauce
30ml/2 tbsp plain (all-purpose) flour
150ml/¼ pint/⅔ cup hot, well-flavoured
  chicken stock
salt and ground black pepper

1 Heat the oil in a large frying pan. Add the bacon and fry until crisp, stirring occasionally. Add the sliced onions to the pan and cook for about 10 minutes, stirring frequently, or until softened.

2 Add the mushrooms and cook lightly for a further 1 minute, stirring well.

3 Use a slotted spoon to remove the bacon and vegetables from the pan and keep warm.

4 Add the liver to the fat remaining in the pan and cook over a high heat for 3–4 minutes, turning once to seal the slices on both sides. Remove the liver from the pan and keep warm.

5 Melt the butter in the pan, add the soy sauce and flour and blend together. Stir in the stock and bring to the boil, stirring until thickened.

6 Return the liver, vegetables and bacon to the pan and heat through for 1 minute. Season to taste, and serve with new potatoes and green beans.

Energy 418kcal/1739kJ; Protein 34.2g; Carbohydrate 9.3g, of which sugars 2.6g; Fat 27.3g, of which saturates 9.5g; Cholesterol 527mg; Calcium 34mg; Fibre 1.3g; Sodium 1257mg.

Pork sausage stew

This hearty casserole, made with meaty sausages and haricot beans, is flavoured with fragrant fresh herbs and dry Italian wine. Serve with crusty bread for mopping up the delicious juices. Remember to leave time for the beans to soak before cooking.

Serves four

225g/8oz/1½ cups dried haricot
   (navy) beans
2 sprigs fresh thyme
30ml/2 tbsp olive oil
450g/1lb pork sausages
1 onion, finely chopped
2 sticks celery, finely diced
300ml/½ pint/1¼ cups dry red or white wine,
   preferably Italian
1 sprig of fresh rosemary
1 bay leaf
300ml/½ pint/1¼ cups boiling
   vegetable stock
200g/7oz can chopped tomatoes
¼ head dark green cabbage, such as cavolo
   nero or Savoy, finely shredded
salt and ground black pepper
chopped fresh thyme, to garnish

4 Fry the onion and celery gently for 5 minutes until softened but not coloured. Add the wine, rosemary and bay leaf and bring to the boil. Then pour the mixture into the casserole. Add the stock and season with pepper. Cover and place in the oven for 2 hours, until the beans are just tender.

Variations
• Try sausages flavoured with garlic (Toulouse-style) or with leeks and sage in this casserole.
• Alternatively, buy Polish boiling sausage (wiejska) from the deli counter and cut it into chunks.

5 Stir the tomatoes and the cabbage into the stew. Cover and cook for 30 minutes, or until the cabbage is tender but not overcooked. Divide among warmed plates or large bowls. Garnish with a little chopped fresh thyme and serve with crusty Italian bread.

1 Put the haricot beans in a large bowl and cover with cold water. Leave to soak for at least 8 hours or overnight.

2 Drain the beans and place in a pan with the thyme and at least twice their volume of cold water. Bring to the boil and boil steadily for 10 minutes, then drain and place in a deep ovenproof casserole, discarding the thyme.

3 Preheat the oven to 160°C/325°F/ Gas 3. Heat the oil in a frying pan and cook the sausages until browned all over. Transfer to the casserole and tip away any excess fat from the pan.

Energy 620kcal/2593kJ; Protein 28.4g; Carbohydrate 47.4g, of which sugars 9.9g; Fat 30.9g, of which saturates 10.8g; Cholesterol 67.5mg; Calcium 205mg; Fibre 7.6g; Sodium 1139mg.

Sweet-and-sour pork

Originally created by the Chinese, sweet-and-sour cooking is now popular the world over. This version has a fresh, clean taste with pineapple for sweetness and Thai fish sauce for contrast. It makes an excellent meal served over rice or noodles.

Serves four

350g/12oz lean pork
30ml/2 tbsp vegetable oil
4 garlic cloves, thinly sliced
1 small red onion, sliced
30ml/2 tbsp Thai fish sauce (nam pla)
15ml/1 tbsp sugar
1 red (bell) pepper, seeded and diced
½ cucumber, seeded and sliced
2 plum tomatoes, cut into wedges
115g/4oz piece of fresh pineapple, cut into
    small chunks
2 spring onions (scallions), cut into
    short lengths
ground black pepper
coriander (cilantro) leaves, to garnish
spring onions (scallions), shredded, to garnish

1 Place the pork in the freezer for 30–40 minutes, until firm. Using a sharp knife, cut it into thin strips.

2 Heat the oil in a wok or large frying pan. Add the garlic. Cook over a medium heat until golden, then add the pork and stir-fry for about 4–5 minutes. Add the red onion slices and toss to mix together.

3 Add the fish sauce, sugar and pepper to taste. Toss the mixture over the heat for 3–4 minutes more, until everything is thoroughly coated.

4 Stir in the red pepper, cucumber, tomatoes, pineapple and spring onions. Stir-fry for 3–4 minutes more, then spoon into a bowl. Garnish with the coriander and spring onions and serve.

Energy 727kcal/3035kJ; Protein 32.7g; Carbohydrate 76.5g, of which sugars 39.4g; Fat 32.8g, of which saturates 5.8g; Cholesterol 272mg; Calcium 85mg; Fibre 2.7g; Sodium 1048mg.

Pork with chickpeas

This is a basic meat and legume casserole that could equally well be made with lamb or poultry, using red kidney or flageolet beans. Diced celery, carrots and mushrooms can also be added. Serve with some warm crusty bread for a hearty meal.

Serves four

350g/12oz/1¾ cups dried chickpeas, soaked
    overnight in water to cover
75–90ml/5–6 tbsp extra virgin olive oil
675g/1½lb boneless leg of pork, cut into
    large cubes
1 large onion, sliced
2 garlic cloves, chopped
400g/14oz can chopped tomatoes
grated rind of 1 orange
1 small dried red chilli (optional)
salt and ground black pepper

1 Drain the chickpeas, rinse under cold water and drain again. Place them in a large pan. Pour in enough cold water to cover generously and bring to the boil. Boil the chickpeas for 10 minutes.

2 Skim any frothy scum off the water. Add more boiling water from a kettle to cover the chickpeas if necessary. Reduce the heat and cover the pan. Simmer the chickpeas for 1–1½ hours or until tender.

3 When the chickpeas are soft and tender, drain them, reserving the cooking liquid, and set them aside.

4 Heat the olive oil in the clean pan and brown the cubes of pork in small batches, so that the fat stays hot and fries the meat rather than stewing it. As each batch browns, lift the meat out with a slotted spoon and set aside.

5 When all the meat is browned, add the onion to the oil remaining in the pan and sauté the onion until light golden.

6 Stir in the garlic, then as soon as it becomes aromatic, add the tomatoes and orange rind. Crumble in the chilli, if using and stir well.

COOK'S TIPS
• Add canned chickpeas 30 minutes before the end of cooking.
• The longer the casserole is cooked, the better it tastes, but check it does not dry out.

7 Return the chickpeas and meat to the pan, with enough of the cooking liquid to cover. Add pepper, then cover and simmer for 1 hour, until tender. Stir occasionally and add more liquid if needed. Season before serving.

Energy 654kcal/2743kJ; Protein 56.4g; Carbohydrate 52.4g, of which sugars 9.6g; Fat 25.7g, of which saturates 4.9g; Cholesterol 106mg; Calcium 178mg; Fibre 11.4g; Sodium 164mg.

Desserts and bakes

Those that are sweet-toothed shall not be forgotten. Choose here from a homely, filling traditional dessert such as bread and butter pudding, or indulge yourself with a chocolate gooey cake served with cream that will take you to chocolate heaven. Alternatively, bake some blueberry muffins or chocolate brownies for a teatime break or a delicious snack on the go.

Bread and butter pudding

This dessert is a traditional British favourite that is inexpensive and easy to make, and full of good ingredients. Essentially, it is custard mixture poured over bread and butter, sweetened and baked. There are many richer variations, but the basic recipe is still the best.

Serves four to six

50g/2oz/4 tbsp butter, softened
about 6 large slices of day-old white bread
50g/2oz dried fruit, such as raisins,
    sultanas (golden raisins) or chopped
    dried apricots
40g/1½oz/3 tbsp caster (superfine) sugar
2 large (US extra large) eggs
600ml/1 pint/2½ cups full cream (whole) milk

1 Preheat the oven to 160°C/325°F/ Gas 5. Lightly butter a 1.2-litre/2-pint/ 5-cup ovenproof dish.

2 Butter the slices of bread and cut them into small triangles or squares.

COOK'S TIPS
• Replace the bread with brioche and the milk with cream for a deluxe version.
• Use this recipe to use up bread that is past its best.

3 Arrange half the bread pieces, buttered side up, in the prepared dish and sprinkle the dried fruit and half of the sugar over the top.

4 Arrange the remaining bread slices, again buttered side up, evenly on top of the fruit, covering any gaps that might be visible. Sprinkle the remaining sugar evenly over the top.

5 To make the custard, beat the eggs lightly together, then stir in the milk. Do not worry about any stringy bits of egg white as these will be removed.

6 Strain the egg mixture and pour it over the bread in the dish. Push the top slices down into the liquid, if necessary, so that it is evenly absorbed.

7 Leave the pudding to stand for 30 minutes to allow the bread to soak up all the liquid.

8 Put the dish into the hot oven and bake for about 45 minutes or until the custard is set and the top is crisp and golden brown. Serve the pudding immediately with pouring cream.

Variations
• To make a special occasion chocolate bread and butter pudding, complete steps 1–4, omitting the dried fruit if you wish. Break 150g/5oz dark (bittersweet) chocolate into 500ml/17fl oz/ generous 2 cups milk and heat gently (on the stove or on low power in the microwave) until the milk is warm and the chocolate has melted. Stir frequently during heating and do not allow the milk to boil. Stir the warm chocolate milk into the beaten eggs in step 5, and then continue with the remaining steps.
• You could replace the dried fruit in either version of the pudding with slices of fresh banana.

Energy 622kcal/2597kJ; Protein 10.5g; Carbohydrate 55.6g, of which sugars 37.8g; Fat 39g, of which saturates 23g; Cholesterol 186mg; Calcium 203mg; Fibre 1.6g; Sodium 350mg.

Chocolate gooey cake

For perfect results it is essential to undercook this cake so that it is dense in the middle. Made with almonds instead of flour, the mixture does not rise and set into the usual cake-like texture.

Serves eight

115g/4oz dark (bittersweet) chocolate
5ml/1 tsp water
115g/4oz/½ cup unsalted (sweet)
 butter, diced
2 eggs, separated
175g/6oz/1½ cups ground almonds
5ml/1 tsp vanilla sugar

COOK'S TIP
Make vanilla sugar by decanting a quantity of caster (superfine) sugar into a jar. Add a vanilla pod (bean), seal and leave for the pod to infuse the sugar.

---

1 Preheat the oven to 180°C/350°F/ Gas 4. Grease a 20cm/8in shallow round cake tin (pan).

2 Break the chocolate into a pan. Add the water and heat gently until the chocolate has melted. Add the butter to the chocolate and stir until melted.

3 Remove from the heat, then add the egg yolks, ground almonds and vanilla sugar. Whisk the egg whites until stiff, then fold them into the chocolate mixture.

4 Spread the mixture gently into the prepared tin and bake in the oven for 15–17 minutes until just set. The mixture should still be soft in the centre. Leave to cool in the tin. When cold, serve with a dollop of lightly whipped double cream, if you like.

Energy 311kcal/1288kJ; Protein 6.8g; Carbohydrate 10g, of which sugars 9.3g; Fat 27.4g, of which saturates 9.9g; Cholesterol 75mg; Calcium 66.2mg; Fibre 1.9g; Sodium 97mg.

Tiramisu

There are many versions of this popular Italian dessert, but all use minimal ingredients and are quick and easy to make. Make it the day before you will eat it so that it is well chilled and set.

Serves six to eight

3 eggs, separated
450g/1lb/2 cups mascarpone, at room
    temperature
10ml/2 tsp vanilla sugar
175ml/6fl oz/¾ cup cold, very strong,
    black coffee
120ml/4fl oz/½ cup coffee-flavoured liqueur
18 savoiardi (Italian sponge fingers)
sifted unsweetened cocoa powder and grated
    dark (bittersweet) chocolate, to finish

1 With an electric mixer, whisk the egg whites until they stand in stiff peaks.

2 Whisk the mascarpone, vanilla sugar and egg yolks in a separate large bowl until evenly combined. Fold in the egg whites. Spread a few spoonfuls of mixture evenly into a large bowl.

Variation
Use Madeira cake cut into slices in place of the savoiardi, if you like.

3 Mix the coffee and liqueur together in a shallow dish. Dip a sponge finger in the mixture, turn it quickly so that it becomes saturated but does not disintegrate, and place it on top of the mascarpone in the bowl. Add five more dipped sponge fingers, placing them side by side.

4 Spoon in about one-third of the remaining mixture and spread it out. Make more layers in the same way, ending with mascarpone. Level the surface, then sift cocoa powder all over. Cover and chill overnight. Before serving, sprinkle with cocoa and grated chocolate.

Energy 215kcal/894kJ; Protein 8.5g; Carbohydrate 12.4g, of which sugars 10.2g; Fat 13.3g, of which saturates 5.9g; Cholesterol 118mg; Calcium 22mg; Fibre 0.1g; Sodium 48mg.

Chocolate brownies

These brownies are packed with milk and dark chocolate, making them rich and intense rather than too sweet. Serve them in small squares, either cold or warm.

Makes sixteen

300g/12oz plain (semisweet) chocolate
300g/12oz milk chocolate
175g/6oz/¾ cup unsalted (sweet) butter
75g/3oz/⅔ cup self-raising (self-rising) flour
3 large (US extra large) eggs

COOK'S TIPS
• The brownies are fabulous for dessert with scoops of good ice cream or white chocolate sauce.
• Try them warm, drizzled with maple syrup.
• Melt 225g/8oz white chocolate in a heatproof bowl set over a small pan of simmering water. Stir in 225g/8oz mascarpone for a rich and dreamy topping.

---

1 Preheat the oven to 180°C/350°F/ Gas 4. Line the base and sides of a 20cm/8in square cake tin (pan) with baking parchment.

2 Break the plain chocolate and 90g/3½oz of the milk chocolate into pieces and put in a heatproof bowl with the butter. Melt over a pan of barely simmering water, stirring frequently.

3 Chop the remaining milk chocolate. Stir the flour and eggs into the melted chocolate. Stir in half the chopped chocolate and turn the mixture into the tin, spreading it evenly. Sprinkle with the remaining chopped chocolate.

4 Bake for 30–35 minutes, until risen and firm. Cool in the tin, then cut into squares. Store in an airtight container.

Energy 297kcal/1239kJ; Protein 3.7g; Carbohydrate 30.2g, of which sugars 21.4g; Fat 18.8g, of which saturates 4.2g; Cholesterol 38mg; Calcium 37mg; Fibre 1.1g; Sodium 16mg.

Blueberry muffins

Light and fruity, these well-known American muffins are delicious at any time of day. Serve them warm for breakfast or brunch, as a tea-time treat or with scoops of ice cream for dessert.

Makes twelve

2 eggs
50g/2oz/4 tbsp butter, melted
175ml/6fl oz/¾ cup milk
5ml/1 tsp vanilla extract
5ml/1 tsp grated lemon rind
180g/6¼oz/generous 1¼ cups plain
  (all-purpose) flour
60g/2¼oz/generous ¼ cup sugar
10ml/2 tsp baking powder
pinch of salt
175g/6oz/1¼ cups fresh blueberries

1 Preheat the oven to 200°C/400°F/ Gas 6. Arrange 12 paper cases in a muffin pan or grease the pan.

2 In a bowl, whisk the eggs until blended. Add the melted butter, milk, vanilla and lemon rind, and stir well to combine.

3 Sift the flour, sugar, baking powder and salt into a bowl. Make a well in the centre and pour in the egg mixture. Stir to combine with a metal spoon.

Variations
• Frozen fruit also works well in the muffins. Try frozen raspberries, blackberries or strawberries instead of blueberries.
• Rhubarb is good in muffins: use small young sticks and cut them into slices about 5mm/¼in thick.

4 Add the blueberries to the muffin mixture and gently fold in.

5 Carefully spoon the batter into the muffin cases, leaving enough space at the top of each for the muffins to rise.

6 Bake for 20–25 minutes, until the risen tops spring back when pressed lightly with a fingertip. Leave the muffins in the pan, if using, for 5 minutes before turning out on to a wire rack to cool.

COOK'S TIPS
• Take care not to over-mix the batter. This toughens the mixture and tends to break up the fruit, resulting in dense muffins.
• If you want to serve the muffins warm for breakfast, weigh out and prepare the dry ingredients the night before to save time.

Energy 127kcal/536kJ; Protein 3.3g; Carbohydrate 18.6g, of which sugars 7.1g; Fat 5g, of which saturates 2.7g; Cholesterol 48mg; Calcium 56mg; Fibre 1g; Sodium 96mg.

Index